Dem Dry Bones

Dem Dry Bones

Preaching, Death, and Hope

Luke A. Powery

Fortress Press
Minneapolis

DEM DRY BONES
Preaching, Death, and Hope

Unless otherwise noted, scripture quotations are the author's own translation or
from the New Revised Standard Version Bible, copyright © 1989 by the Division of
Christian Education of the National Council of Churches of Christ in the USA, and
are used with permission.

Cover design: Alisha Lofgren
Cover image: *Valley of the Dry Bones* © James Nesbitt

Library of Congress Cataloging-in-Publication Data

Powery, Luke A., 1974-
Dem dry bones : preaching, death, and hope / Luke A. Powery.
    p. cm.
Includes bibliographical references (p.   ) and index.
ISBN 978-0-8006-9822-5 (pbk. : alk. paper) -- ISBN 978-1-4514-2439-3
(ebook)
1. Preaching. 2. African American preaching. 3. Bible. O.T. Ezekiel XXXVII--
    Criticism, interpretation, etc. 4. Spirituals (Songs)--History and criticism
    5. Hope--Religious aspects--Christianity. 6. Death--Religious aspects--
Christianity. 7. Holy Spirit. I. Title.
BV4208.U6P68 2012
251--dc23
                            2012011672

The paper used in this publication meets the minimum requirements of American
National Standard for Information Sciences—Permanence of Paper for Printed
Library Materials, ANSI Z329.48-1984.

Manufactured in the U.S.A.

16   15   2   3   4   5   6   7   8   9   10

For Gail

Till death do us part

Contents

Preface

The spoken and sung word formed the spiritual air that I breathed in the home of my parents. But one afternoon on 216th Street in Bronx, New York, I struggled to physically breathe and convulsed in my mother's arms due to a very high fever. One of my brothers had just arrived home from school and saw what was happening. He called my father while crying and said, "Luke is dead." The medical team said that I was "out for fifteen minutes." Death touched me as an infant, though I do not remember the incident, and it is a touch that never really goes away. I face my mortality with humility and recognize that my present dying helps me in my living.

The sting of death, however, was matched with the song of life, also as a baby. My parents tell me that at eleven months old I could whistle and would do so to our neighbor from a third-floor window of our home. This musical inclination has never left me either, so I sing on. This look backward brings me forward to this exploration of the spirituals as a way to study the intersection of singing and death, which has its roots in the soil of my childhood's soul.

This book on the spirituals, preaching, death, and hope is the second installment in an informal series that I call "traces of the Spirit"; the first was *Spirit Speech: Lament and Celebration in Preaching*. Both works draw upon African diasporan cultural sources to do theological work in the field of homiletics. Both deal with the Spirit's work in relation to suffering, thus taking God and human suffering seriously in the practice of preaching. This work takes up the spirituals of enslaved blacks in the United States in particular. These religious folk songs have historically been called the "Negro spirituals" and in modern times "African American spirituals." Because of the politics of naming and racial categorization, I have opted to refer to these songs created during slavery just as the enslaved did by primarily calling them "spirituals" throughout the book (though sometimes I may refer to them as "African American spirituals").

For this project, I used primarily the spiritual lyrics from three sources: *Slave Songs of the United States: The Classic 1867 Anthology*, eds. William Francis Allen et al.; James Weldon Johnson and J. Rosamond Johnson's *The Books of American Negro Spirituals*, 2 vols.; and *Songs of Zion*. Other sources could have been utilized and been just as effective. Because the spirituals must be heard and not just read or discussed, I recommend consulting the bibliographies in the works noted throughout this book, specifically for audio/visual materials about the spirituals.

These literary resources cannot compare to the human resources that have encouraged me on this journey. Word-count limits prohibit me from saying all that needs to be said. But "in-a my heart" I sing a Eucharist for all who have supported this endeavor. I thank Princeton Theological Seminary for the sabbatical year in which most of this book was written; President Iain Torrance and Dean James Kay, along with other colleagues, particularly those in the practical theology department, have been a wellspring of support. Also, I thank the community of Yale Divinity School for their hospitality while I served as a Visiting Fellow during my sabbatical; the homileticians there, Nora Tisdale and Tom Troeger, were wonderful conversation partners and life-giving wells. Tom, the theo-musical homiletician, even reviewed some of my chapter drafts. I thank the Wabash Center for supporting financially some of the research for this project as well as Yolanda Pierce for lively conversations about this research. There are countless others in the heavenly and earthly cloud of witnesses who could be thanked. You know who you are. I will be forever grateful to those institutions, churches, and conferences where I had the opportunity over the last few years to present some of the ideas in this book. The questions raised and comments made influenced this work for the better. The research assistance of Joy Harris and Ashley Brown also made my task lighter. I would be remiss if I did not thank my extraordinary editor, David Lott, who was a constant joy with whom to work, always open to chat or e-mail; he gave me hope that the bones of this book would actually fit together as a whole! Last, I am indebted to my family—Gail, Moriah, and Zachary. Without their loving support, this book would have never been born. Like the spiritual, they make me say "Glory, Hallelujah!"

In the Middle of a Valley

The Need of Preaching

. . . he brought me out by the spirit of the Lord and set me down in the middle of a valley . . .

—EZEK. 37:1

Go down in de lonesome valley, To meet my Jesus dere.

—TRADITIONAL

Much of the writing of this book took place with a clear view of death. Through the large glass windows of the Princeton Public Library on Paul Robeson Place in Princeton, New Jersey, I gazed at the Princeton Cemetery of the Nassau Presbyterian Church where the "many thousand gone" rested. I felt that to write about preaching and death, I had to have enough courage to face death regularly. Thus I chose to reflect on preaching and its relationship to death and hope while looking at the tombstones of a great cloud of witnesses. In this cemetery, many well-known persons such as Jonathan Edwards lie alongside countless others whose names are not famous, though they, too, struggled in the fight against death.

To look at the vast impact of death symbolized in this cemetery challenged me to consider whether I really believed in the resurrection of the dead and preaching resurrection hope. Is there any hope among death's ashes? Through those library windows, I saw death's sting and the grave's apparent victory. I chose to write about preaching, death, and hope in the face of death because I knew that if I was not ready to face death, I was not ready to preach life and hope or even ready to discuss it. Facing death taught me about the life of the ministry of preaching. John Witvliet puts it this way: "For the living, there is no better antidote to arrogant, sloppy living than intentional visits to a funeral home, a walk through a cemetery, or attendance at a funeral. Rule number one for thoughtful living: Do not miss a funeral."[1] Likewise, an antidote to sloppy preaching and a key rule for thoughtful preaching is to face the reality of death daily. This means preaching must entail pain and suffering even though this is not popular with numerous Christians who only want their souls massaged and not strengthened, resulting in a type of preaching that promotes profits for speaker and listener (most certainly for the preachers) and a particular theological school of thought controlling the homiletical airwaves.

"Candy" Theology in Contemporary Preaching

Preaching has become a big business in a good deal of today's Christendom. Glamour and glitz glare through various media forms as some preachers pimp the gospel for financial profits. When high-tech marketing or branding of a certain type of spiritual beauty dominates, then "an aesthetic of prosperity becomes an ethic of prosperity."[2] In this spiritual marketing strategy, the flaunting of one's material wealth and physical health is a validation of the Christian faith. This so-called prosperity gospel, which has become an important part of North American Christianity, is a version of consumer culture. Thus it is believed that the more one possesses materially, the more it is obvious that one is blessed by God and is doing God's will. Because of this lens of prosperity, one continually asks for more to get more. It is a love affair with more. Marvin McMickle observes in a critical way that, in prosperity-gospel churches, "every passage of scripture [serves] as a passport to a bigger house, a larger car, or an expanding bank account."[3] He questions "the apparent celebration of the exorbitant and self-indulgent lifestyle that is avidly pursued by an increasing number of preachers in America, often as a result of milking and bilking their congregations through some prosperity gospel scheme."[4] McMickle is not alone in his criticism. Robert Franklin declares that the implicit muting of prophetic ministry by the proclamation of prosperity has helped to create a "crisis in the village." He writes, "If most black preachers—and other preachers for that matter—are preoccupied with pursuing the 'bling-bling' life of conspicuous consumption, then poor people are in big trouble."[5] I would add that not just poor people, but anyone experiencing existential pain and suffering on any level is in big trouble.

This theme of prosperity threaded through some preaching also finds its way in the music ministries of many of these congregations such that they emphasize "praise and worship" or celebration without likewise acknowledging lament and death in real life, what Gordon Lathrop calls "little deaths."[6] "Little deaths" foreshadow our last death and reveal how we are dying on a regular basis even in the midst of our living. These little deaths may be physical sickness or disabilities, moments of transition and loss, failures, manifestations of violence, experiences and corrupt systems of injustices, and the like. These deaths occur daily to demonstrate that we are dying a slow death. In many ways, this book, in discussing death, will have in mind these "little deaths" while not ignoring the "big" death at the end of life.[7]

Prosperity preaching seems not to take any type of death seriously as a crucial component of the Christian life. This could be because the prosperity gospel promotes a kind of "pain-free religious experience," according to Stephanie Mitchem.[8] Within its spiritual purview, pain is not a part of prosperity. Critiquing this camp of Christendom, Melissa Harris-Lacewell notes that "Christ is an investment strategy and a personal life coach whose power can be accessed by believers to improve their finances, protect their families, strengthen their faith, and achieve personal authenticity."[9] The power of Christ is accessed for prosperity purposes. There is no place for pain in this gospel strategy. This approach to the Christian faith is not surprising when one considers the core beliefs and practices of a key wing of the prosperity gospel, the Word of Faith movement. At the core of this movement is knowing who you are in Christ, positive confession or mental attitude, and emphasis on material prosperity and wealth and physical health.[10]

Despite the numerous critiques of prosperity preaching, it is still the case that these preachers, in some way, answer a longing of many African Americans and others. I say this not to endorse this "pain-free" preaching enterprise but to highlight the complexities that are involved. For a people who have been disenfranchised economically and socially for centuries, prosperity preaching can be appealing. It offers a message of personal and individual empowerment for those who desire upward mobility in society. The prosperity message can be viewed as an "ideology of socioeconomic transition"[11] that meets the longing of many who want to achieve success and social acceptance. This "spirituality of longing" finds its answer in "prosperity as realized spirituality," the concretization of a faith rooted in overcoming social rejection by accumulating wealth.[12] Monetary cash flow is implied to be that which can fill spiritual emptiness and quiet the longing in a hurting people. The problem with this approach is the perception that God is a Santa Claus delivering monetary gifts to consuming children who always want more than they have. In addition, the biblical witness asserts that "the love of money is the root of all kinds of evil" (1 Tim. 6:10), suggesting that prosperity preaching may be leading some Christians down the wrong path.

In a prosperity-driven ecclesial environment, whenever the community gathers it is primarily as a means toward greater health and wealth, to get more. "Mo' money, mo' money, mo' money" takes on new religious meaning in this setting. But the obvious tension with all of this is that this prosperity gospel appears to meet the needs of people in the pews, at least on the surface. One cannot deny that masses of people adhere to the prosperity gospel; its permeating presence on different media outlets evidences its popularity. Prosperity proclamation has a huge following and those who subscribe to this message should not be castigated for it. After all, who would not want "Your Best Life Now"[13] in this world when all one has possibly known is suffering? As Jonathan Walton says, "Though in my mind God offered liberation from racial and gender injustice and capitalist exploitation, I saw other preachers seemingly get further with a Jesus who provided the keys to the Kingdom in the form of a four-bedroom house and a Mercedes-Benz."[14] For have-nots, to finally have something, especially in the way just described, could be perceived as a divinely sanctioned physical blessing. The issue becomes what it means to "get further" with Jesus, that is, what it means to live the life of Christian discipleship, including the content of our proclamation.

Popular prosperity Christianity is just that, popular, partly because of what has been called "teleconditioning."[15] This is where one's Christian faith is conditioned by what is viewed through television and the Internet. The perceived prosperity of the preachers validates their message. As noted, the aesthetic leads to an ethic of prosperity that becomes the heart of the adhered-to gospel. In a 2006 *Religion and Ethics Newsweekly* interview, legendary prince of the pulpit Gardner Taylor was asked to assess the current preaching scene. What he says is illuminating for this book's conversation:

> there is now a tendency, I think, more than ever, to make [preaching] a kind of Sunday Chamber of Commerce exercise—motivational speaking, which has its place but is not the Gospel. It becomes a kind of opium, if opium is a stimulant, for people, which gives them often a false notion of what life is all about. I think much of contemporary preaching does not prepare people for the inevitable crises of life. When we talk constantly about prosperity, well, life is not constantly prosperity. It has adversity and difficulties, and if one is trained, conditioned to see only the bright side of things, then one is not prepared for living in this world.
>
> . . . Of course, people want to hear it, because candy is a very pleasant thing. . . . When [my daughter] was a little girl, I suppose we could have fed her candy morning, noon, and night, and she would have taken it morning, noon—and enjoyed it. Soon she would have had no teeth, and soon we would have had no daughter, I think, because candy is wonderful. I love it, but one needs in one's diet more than candy.[16]

Taylor's notion that a prosperity-only message is like "candy" suggests that this type of theology and preaching is initially sweet to the taste, a "pleasant thing," but in the end it is detrimental because life is not just about the "bright side of things." If one chews on this prosperity message long enough, one will end up with "no teeth" because "one needs in one's diet more than candy." Prosperity preaching may be sweet like a candy cane at first but it will eventually be sour for the soul and bad for one's spiritual teeth and nerve. "Candy" homiletical theology does not sustain people's lives in the end because it does not take into consideration "what life is all about." The hardships and pain of life tend to be muted in this bright, sunny gospel. It is a false, distorted picture of the gospel if death and sorrow are ignored. Prosperity preaching does not engage the valleys of life truthfully but only "name and claim" the mountaintops of the high life. Yet in the valley of the shadow of death, God can also be found. "Thou art with me," the psalmist says (Psalm 23, KJV). Furthermore, God may even be the one who leads us to the valley, the valley of dry bones, death (Ezek. 37). The prosperity gospel proclaims a hope but its version of hope erases death. This, in fact, is not hope at all, because Christian hope is not hope without death. Real hope is discovered in the midst of death, created on the anvil of adversity.

Denying Death in a Context of Death

One of the major flaws of prosperity preaching is its attempt to proclaim hope while avoiding or denying death. To follow Jesus Christ through our Christian preaching does not equate to proclaiming bigger and better material goods; rather, it involves taking up crosses and following him in his death and life. Preaching entails truthfulness about his crucifixion and resurrection, his death and life, and the hope found in him. To follow Jesus through our preaching means that one must take suffering seriously. Thus one cannot preach prosperity hope without being honest about human pain and agony, about "little deaths." I do not aim to denigrate this prosperity-gospel segment of the church but I do want to highlight what I think is a huge theological hole in this form of proclamation and any other contemporary approach to preaching that avoids dealing with death substantively.

Within prosperity-gospel teaching, pain of varied kinds is deemed a problem, stemming from a person's lack of faith or the devil. Shayne Lee notes, "Word-of-faith teaching asserts that Christians have the power to control their physical well-being and financial fortunes through their faith. . . . However, God's 'hands are tied' from blessing many Christians who lack faith and misappropriate biblical principles, thus explaining why all Christians are not experiencing prosperous and healthy lives."[17] Wealth and health are the proper inheritance for God's children. If this material and physical prosperity are absent, it is the individual's fault in some way or the devil is at work. The realization of systemic sin through structures that keep the poor poor and others oppressed is not even acknowledged. There is a clear disregard for or ignorance of what Chuck Campbell calls the "powers of death."[18] Rather, positive confession and right faith with proper handling of the Scriptures is the right equation to win the prosperity lotto. Some do see a "glimmer of hope"[19] in this type of gospel preaching; but, at the same time, one of the harshest criticisms of this doctrine is how it implies the condemnation of those who are not healthy and wealthy. Sometimes, tornados blow through the valley of life and it is no one's fault or due to a lack of faith. Sickness and suffering come as a part of what it means to be human in a broken world. This is often denied in a pain-free preaching approach. The perceived glimmer of hope through prosperity preaching is actually a false sense of hope because of its disconnection from the crucible of life. Christian hope grows within and without of the crucible of death. Any preaching that denies death will ultimately be hopeless because it does not engage earthly realities.

Even those who feed their souls through prosperity preaching discover sometimes that a fuller gospel should be proclaimed. Marla Frederick interviewed African American women who watch prosperity televangelists and discovered a form of discontentment among them. In one case, she states, "While popular television ministers might boast of multimillion dollar homes, women in the viewing audience . . . often must negotiate their interpretations of prosperity against the limited resources of their communities."[20] The negotiation happens because the prosperity preachers preach a gospel that is detached from "little deaths," our human reality that includes such things as limited resources. In another interview, one woman announces her discontentment with Creflo Dollar's message:

> You know every time I hear him, it's the same thing. . . . You know sometimes you need to hear something more than prosperity. You know you're going through some things and there's some other things that you're dealing with in your life. . . . You know, something spiritual. . . . You know, not just always prospering. So, that's why I stopped listening to him. . . . But, it's not that I didn't like his ministry. It's just that at different times in your life you need other Word coming forth.[21]

What this woman reveals is the conflict between the preached word and her life. Basically, a need was not being met through the prosperity message. There was a divide between her Christian life and the Christian life that was preached because, as she acknowledges, one goes "through some things." Life is "not just always prospering." "Sometimes you need to hear something more than prosperity." Why? It is because human life includes pain and suffering, too, and the prosperity gospel denies their role in Christian discipleship, viewing them as something to be ignored or denied. It is at least a "masking of mortality"[22] and human struggle. Little deaths are relegated as part of human faithlessness or blamed as the devil's doing. I believe this is the case because preachers in this context do not know what else to say nor does their theological framework allow for the ways in which death is a part of life. Tom Long claims in relation to funerals that "Americans are no longer sure what to do with our dead."[23] This ambiguity over or discomfort with the dead is also an indication about how in our preaching we do not know what to do with the dying present in our everyday living, the little deaths. What is clear is that the prosperity homiletical approach is inadequate to meet the needs of struggling individuals and communities because human experience includes tough realities for many. Life in the middle of a valley reveals that death is all around. Preaching that ignores this will eventually fail and not do the ministry it was commissioned to do.

Preaching has many aims, one of which is to minister to the felt needs of people.[24] The world is brewing with ongoing trouble—war, famine, genocide, governmental corruption, economic instability, to name a few. To ignore these expressions of death is to be homiletically blind and irrelevant. In African American communities alone, the existential devastation is vast. There are megachurches that preach a mini-gospel at times, one that promotes a feel-good religion. Yet the people in the pews and in the surrounding communities are not always feeling good because that is not the earthly reality. As McMickle observes, there are numerous black congregations that are located in neighborhoods resembling "bombed-out war zones."[25] Drugs, alcoholism, HIV/AIDS, prostitution, domestic violence, and rising poverty rates among children pervade many urban communities.

I preach monthly at a Presbyterian church in Newark, New Jersey. The building is large but the congregation is small. This is a church whose "glory days" have blown away in the wind of a changing demographic in that particular community. The good ol' days of economic prosperity and social safety in the neighborhood have passed. This church and neighborhood are in transition and are struggling to survive. In this mostly African American and Latino/a neighborhood, "little deaths" are all around as police sirens sound during many sermons. What kind of power would a prosperity gospel have in this setting without dealing with the concrete realities in that community? Death stares at this congregation in the form of a crack house across the street, while preachers declare the cross of Christ faithfully. In the proclamation of the cross, one has to name human pain, even the agony of Christ. This naming is important to overcoming not only the "crisis in the village" but the "crisis in the pulpit." Robert Franklin argues that "leaders who are unaware of, or uncomfortable with engaging and addressing, the pain of the people are unlikely to mobilize the power of the people."[26] Individuals should be mobilized for public service in society, not for personal gain and prosperity. Public service is vital as an outcome of life-giving preaching, especially in light of existential suffering in black communities and other segments of the global society. But this service stems from preachers truthfully naming the realities of death.

In light of the heartbreaking realities, these "specters of death,"[27] it is preposterous that some preachers can separate the gospel from the presence of death in the world as a way of avoiding it in the pulpit. Preaching itself is a part of a larger liturgical framework permeated by images and symbols of death. Through the rite of baptism, we die and rise with Christ (Rom. 6:4-5). Baptism is life but it is also a death. Baptism by immersion depicts this well as a new convert is submerged, buried, under the water, and then raised out of the water. Likewise, communion is a table of death and life. In the words of the apostle Paul, "for as often as you eat this bread and drink the cup, you proclaim the Lord's death until he comes" (1 Cor. 11:26). The Eucharist proclaims a death. At the heart of Christian worship is death. This is unavoidable, though many times not accented or recognized. As Witvliet writes, "We all live under a death sentence."[28] This is revealed through our liturgies. But this should not be a shock because Christianity is about a Jewish man who died and eventually conquered death. More will be said about this later; for now, it suffices to uncover the stench of death that permeates the communal worship in which preaching happens.

Furthermore, various historical accounts in which literal deaths transpired during a worship experience poignantly demonstrate the fusion of death and worship. Archbishop Oscar Romero of El Salvador was assassinated while he presided at the Eucharist. The founder of the Taizé community in France, Brother Roger, was fatally stabbed to death by a mentally ill woman during a prayer service; his hospitality killed him. Alberta King, the mother of Dr. Martin Luther King Jr., had her life stolen by a sniper's bullet while playing smooth harmonies on the Hammond organ at Ebenezer Baptist Church in Atlanta. Corporate worship can be bloody, figuratively or literally, as these accounts show, but many times in the North American context, worship, including preaching, is sanitized and highly commercialized, as in the case of prosperity ministries and other consumer-oriented groups. Death is muted and even quarantined from the worship experience.

However, these existential and liturgical realities demonstrate that death is prominent as a context for preaching. Death has historically been denied in culture and "alienated from the normal compass of daily experience."[29] Preachers have followed this trajectory by alienating death and anything that might have its smell from sermons—what might be called the homiletical quarantining of death. But preaching that ignores death is irresponsible, a theological lie, and unable to declare real hope. It is, in fact, Spirit-less preaching. If this approach to preaching is theologically faulty, what then does it mean to preach Christian hope in a meaningful way? It means that one proclaims death.

In order to experience life, resurrection, or hope, one must go through death. In fact, the Spirit leads preachers to a milieu of death each Sunday in order to proclaim a word of life that ultimately breathes hope into the lives of people. Yet, in many contemporary churches, some preachers avoid dealing with death because they do not realize its vital connection to the substance of Christian hope. Because of this denial of death, we are left with sermons that possess a weak pneumatology and are fundamentally hopeless.

Telling the Gospel Truth

The purpose of this book is to remedy some of the theological and homiletical shortcomings in contemporary preaching by probing the concept of death as a critical aspect of the meaning of Christian hope. Preaching hope is inadequate without taking death seriously. Not only is death the context for preaching hope, but hope is generated by experiencing death through the Spirit who is the ultimate source of hope. Death is placed in the foreground not to celebrate death but to accentuate the resilient power of life and hope. By affirming death as necessary for preaching Christian hope, I imply that giving hope is a key, if not one of the most important, purpose of preaching. Interestingly, in one book about "key terms in homiletics"[30] and in another about "the purposes of preaching,"[31] the theme of hope is missing. Maybe this signals how hopeless Christian preaching has become. This is not to suggest that no one discusses hope in preaching, as some do, but even these treatments are not sustained and lack substantive explorations that integrate death into the conceptualization of hope. In addition, homiletical literature that reflects on death and preaching is limited and much of what is written has only to do with funerals or Christology.[32] These are important, yet this book not only attempts to bridge death and hope in constructive ways but asserts that death is more than an event at the end of someone's life; death is a part of life as "little deaths," as discussed above. This study endeavors to be a sustained treatment of the relationship of death and hope in preaching and it does so by drawing on African American resources in particular, namely the spirituals, of which I will soon say more.

One could frame this vital conversation in the wake of Japan's 2011 tsunami or Haiti's 2010 earthquake and ask, "What does it mean to preach amid the rubble?" or "How can one preach in devastating situations?" Of course, many communities and individuals have not experienced any earthquakes or tsunamis in their entire existence, and especially not with such an aftermath as in Haiti, for example—sidewalk graves, dead bodies in the streets, people setting up home on the street, mothers weeping and gnashing teeth over lost children, or being trapped under a slab of cement from a collapsed building. However, it is possible that someone's life in any congregation is in shambles because a metaphoric earthquake has hit their life, making it a valley of dry bones. Many people in the pews are in the middle of their own valleys for various reasons.

In a church where I once served as a pastor, there was a woman named Rose. Rose and I sat in a restaurant to share a meal together. She told me about her relationship with her husband and how he had abused her and her daughter for many years and yet she remained married to him. At one point in the conversation, after hearing the horrific stories and seeing the tears of pain drop from her face, I said to her, "That's not living." Rose said, "Luke, I died a long time ago." She was a part of the walking dead. Her situation represents many parishioners who are already dead or are dying in various ways. People like Rose come every Sunday to church for a word from the Lord. They are dead and are in need of resurrection. Preaching that engages death as a part of preaching hope will reclaim preaching, in the words of James Forbes, as a "ministry of raising the dead."[33] To preach resurrection, we must acknowledge the presence of death, which is what envelops our lives. The resurrection of Christ implies that resurrection "preaching bears in its own fiber a note of victory."[34] There is the hope of the resurrection *and* the death of the crucifixion. But the hope arises out of the death. This is why some refer to the ministry of preaching as a "burdensome joy."[35] The acknowledgment of death in life is the burden along with the embrace of the responsibility of the call to preach, but joy comes when resurrection life overwhelms death with the realization that God can use feeble human gifts to raise others to newness of life. The gospel includes both dying and living, death and hope. Perhaps this is what leads Gardner Taylor to declare that the preacher's message "involves issues nothing less than those of life and death."[36]

To ascertain the pervasiveness of death in life, even the walking dead, means that preachers have the responsibility to proclaim "the whole counsel of God,"[37] the whole truth of the gospel. A key aspect of the truth is that "Death is something we cannot elude."[38] Kirk Byron Jones reminds us that even "Calvary was not a hoax," thus sometimes preaching becomes "blues preaching,"[39] or what I have called elsewhere "sermonic lament."[40] As an aspect of preaching, the blues means that one proclaims the "gospel as tragedy." Frederick Buechner says that "The Gospel is bad news before it is good news."[41] Good news is not the totality of the gospel; thus to tell the whole gospel truth one must preach the bad news, too. The bad news is the suffering and pain experienced by humanity, the little deaths. Preaching this would hopefully meet the needs of many listeners.

In a 1938 interview, Henry Baker, an ex-slave, provides insight into effective preaching based on his advice to preachers of his day. He says, "I talks ter de preachers en says dat all 'nominations gotter git togedder en center on one thing en dat is de suffering uv de people, 'gardless uv whut nomination or whether dey is even in de church."[42] Baker encourages preachers to focus on the suffering of people and not avoid it as if it does not exist. He wants preachers to be truthful about reality, about the gospel. Suffering is part of the gospel truth. To preach about it may not be comfortable or a delight but, as Mitchem reminds us, "a religion constructed for one's physical comfort ultimately does not assist spiritual maturity . . ."[43] Preaching the whole counsel of God will nurture a mature spiritual life rather than a spirituality that cannot handle death and attempts to hide it. Preaching should not "keep [death] behind a curtain or locked in a closet"[44] any longer but expose its nature in all of its forms. This can be difficult in a death-denying culture in which "Death is not allowed to offer its body in public except through a surreption."[45] By removing the veil over death in our world and naming it, one might actually move closer to preaching hope, for the only way to preach Christian hope is by proclaiming death. This is how one tells the truth of the gospel, the whole truth and nothing but the truth.

Toni Morrison's *Song of Solomon* presents a confrontation between Macon Dead and his son Milkman, where Macon says, "You a big man now, but big ain't nearly enough. You have to be a whole man. And if you want to be a whole man, you have to deal with the whole truth."[46] These words speak deeply to the task of preachers. It is not enough to be a big-name preacher riding in a Bentley. The church needs whole preachers and if one wants to be a whole preacher "you have to deal with the whole truth." The whole gospel truth is that life is real but so is death and death is the context out of which hope grows. Through this study, I will argue that preaching in the Spirit means proclaiming death as an avenue toward hope. In short, no death, no hope. That is the truth I attempt to uncover in this book.

Exploring the Gospel Truth

Spirituals as Primary Source

To assist in the process of telling the gospel truth, I will engage homiletical theory, theology, ethnomusicology, and biblical studies, but there are two important resources that will be particularly helpful in this study. The first are the African American spirituals. Because of the interface of death, hope, and the Spirit, themes very much present in the spirituals, in this study I will explore these historical and cultural musical "sermons" produced in the midst of death as a vital resource for preaching Christian hope. I will examine the history and theology of the spirituals through textual analysis primarily but also be sensitive to their musical soundscape. One could call this whole project a homiletical study of the spirituals.

Several books provide insight into the theological themes of the spirituals, while others are historical or musicological studies. Many of these have been resources for this book, but none provide a homiletical lens. Viewing the spirituals as musical sermons and integrating the spirituals as a significant theological and cultural resource for contemporary preaching makes a distinct contribution to homiletics. No work on preaching explores the spirituals in any substantive fashion with the aim of enhancing the theory and practice of preaching despite the rich historical link between intoned preaching and the spirituals. Thus I hope much fruit will be born from this work.

In particular for this book about preaching, death, and hope, the spirituals are important because the reality of death permeates them. Unlike those who engage death at a distance or not at all, the creators of the spirituals had "immediate, inescapable, dramatic" contact with the dead.[47] These musical sermons were born out of deathly experiences of slavery. Thus a conversation about preaching, death, and hope will be served well by their inclusion. Homiletical lessons about death and hope can be learned from the spirituals. The presence of death is obvious in these songs but so is hope and life, even if simply represented in the phenomenon of singing itself. In his classic text *Black Song,* John Lovell notes, ". . . the African blood has always sung."[48] This singing was a sign of life within environs of death. Despite the blatant hardships, the "haunting overtones"[49] of life and hope rang out. Preachers will do well to pay attention to these songs that preach.

Furthermore, the spirituals provide an opportunity to use African American cultural resources to teach all preachers about preaching. The spirituals may be rightly poised to do this because, as Lovell says, they "dug deep into the universal human heart."[50] They are particular yet speak universally out of that specific setting about the human experience. There is something for everyone in these songs. They are, as W. E. B. Du Bois asserts, the "rhythmic cry of the slave" and "the most beautiful expression of human experience born this side of the seas." Furthermore, he states that the spiritual "still remains as the singular spiritual heritage of the nation and the greatest gift of the Negro people."[51] Though the spirituals are, in the words of James Earl Massey, the "earliest documented world-view of African American spirituality,"[52] they resonate with many people in a variety of cultural contexts. Therefore, this turn to the past for the present is a turn for all preachers who desire to preach Christian hope in a more faithful, robust, and *spiritual* manner.

There have been many debates about the origins of the spirituals and their influences, namely, whether they are imitations of European songs or fully African.[53] This project is not interested in that historical debate but is concerned with the fact that the spirituals tell the gospel truth and can help our preaching tell that truth more faithfully and honestly. The spirituals transgress time, thus they are fruitful for contemporary homiletical reflection. In addition, despite the popularization of the spirituals by the Fisk Jubilee Singers and Hampton Institute Singers through their public concert tours in the past and present, this study attempts to explore the spirituals and imagine their performance from the rugged vantage point of their original context, enslavement and death.[54] Of course, one cannot travel back in time to be in that setting to grasp the original "mood."[55] But what is clear is that these songs were not art music or art for art's sake; they were a matter of life and death created by the unknown black bards.[56] James Weldon Johnson says the bards were "unfamed . . . untaught, unknown, unnamed."[57] This book turns to the so-called unlettered black bards for pearls of homiletical wisdom.

Valley of Dry Bones as Metaphor

In conjunction with the primary sources of the spirituals, the biblical story of the vision of the valley of dry bones in Ezekiel 37 will be another important literary resource for this study on preaching, death, and hope. Ezekiel and the vision of the valley of dry bones has been an important rhetorical trope throughout African American musical and sermonic history. Henry Louis Gates refers to this story as one of the "canonical narratives" within African American experience.[58] Its presence is particularly strong in the history of the practice of black preaching. Allen Callahan notes, "The biblical vision of the valley of bleached bones became a venerable image in African-American preaching."[59] The truth of this is affirmed in the preface to James Weldon Johnson's *God's Trombones*, where he talks about folk sermons that were slightly modified as they were passed on "from preacher to preacher and from locality to locality." One such sermon was "The Valley of Dry Bones" based on Ezekiel 37.[60] This sermonic tradition of a "valley of dry bones" is evident in the preaching of numerous black preachers.[61]

It is obvious from a reading of homiletical history that Ezekiel and the vision of the valley of dry bones has been a sermonic trope in African American settings. This biblical trope has also been present in African American music and other art forms as well. Probably most popular is the spiritual "Dem bones, dem bones, dem dry bones," which focuses on the bones connecting to one another. In addition, Oscar Micheaux's 1925 silent movie *Body and Soul* depicts Paul Robeson as a preacher who proclaims a sermon about Ezekiel and the valley of dry bones, "Dry Bones in the Valley." The intertitle says that this sermon "is a sermon which is every black preacher's ambition,"[62] confirming again the particular prominence of this biblical narrative in preaching. But even certain plays incorporate this biblical trope in their story lines, as August Wilson does in his play *Joe Turner's Come and Gone*, though he uses the watery grave of the Middle Passage instead of the valley of Ezekiel.[63] Nonetheless, this biblical story looms large in various cultural productions within African American contexts.

Perhaps this is not surprising due to the prominent theme of exile in Ezekiel 37, a theme that is particularly relevant for African Americans. In his commentary on the book of Ezekiel, Dexter Callender writes, "The conditions of Jerusalem's deported were different, given that they were largely people of means whose experience was not that of chattel slavery and who retained some control of their economic destiny. . . . Still, their

tradition of exile as emblematic of their experience resonated with sur-
viving victims of the African slave trade, who engaged it in a variety of
ways."[64] The black experience in the Americas can be described as exilic.
Callahan writes, "Ezekiel's wind-swept valley continues to remind slavery's children of their exile. They continue to be strangers in a strange
land. And they continue to be haunted by the bones."[65]

Another reason this biblical vision of the valley of dry bones is so prevalent in African American culture historically could be due to the sense
that God was experienced through the Bible. As Callahan suggests, "The
oracle of God's reviving spirit does not merely recount an event of divine
presence: the words of the text now signify that presence. Ezekiel's lumi-
nous text is the verbal image and likeness of God." This biblical vision is
"iconic."[66] For African Americans, Ezekiel 37 has great importance, especially sermonically, as shown. This trope has been viewed as their experience in exile while still affirming the presence of God in their lives, even
through this particular text. However, there has also been homiletical,
hermeneutical, and musical freedom in relation to this passage because
"neither Negro spirituals nor African-American preaching traditions com-
ment on the Bible's postexilic narratives."[67] Blacks have most assuredly
embraced the dry bones and their coming together but have not invested
their energies in pure reiterations of biblical texts; more will be said about
this later. For now, it suffices to note how significant Ezekiel and the vision
of the valley of dry bones have been in African American preaching and
other forms of communication.

Therefore, this book will embrace this vision of the valley of dry bones
as a metaphor for preaching in the Spirit and as a way of continuing in
this long cultural tradition. Though this biblical story has been used in
the practice of preaching as a trope, I will utilize it for the purpose of
preaching theory, to help foster reflection about the nature and purpose of
preaching today. I desire to reimagine what preaching is because what we
think preaching is shapes how we prepare to preach and how we preach.
Ezekiel and the vision of the valley of dry bones complement the spirituals
such that one is challenged to take death, hope, the Spirit, and preaching
more seriously. Through a conversation with these resources and others,
preaching may regain its spiritual courage and nerve with something more
at stake than a nice whoop or paycheck. When we preach, we preach at the
intersection of life and death. Ezekiel's vision leads us hopefully to become
more interested in a theology of preaching and not just the mere technol-
ogy of preaching.

Through this approach, I affirm the dry bones trope's significant function within African American experience historically. Moreover, such a metaphoric lens suggests a context of death for preaching with the presence of the Spirit restoring hope in God's people. This will become clearer at the outset of each chapter in which I discuss an aspect of this biblical narrative as a theo-biblical entrée into the focus of each chapter.

Movement of This Book

This introduction has attempted to provide the overall rationale for this project on preaching, death, and hope by presenting the perceived problem of contemporary preaching as being the avoidance of dealing forthrightly with death as a part of life and not just primarily in funeral sermons. This is a theo-homiletical problem, especially in light of a contemporary context of death and violence in society on numerous levels, especially in African American communities. The problem is clear and the major purpose of this study is to argue that death is a critical aspect of preaching Christian hope by being in primary conversation with African American spirituals through the metaphorical lens of Ezekiel and the vision of the valley of dry bones. As I suggest, this will help me to tell the gospel truth. The groundwork for this book has been laid in this chapter while the argument will unfold in the following way in the subsequent chapters.

Chapter 1 introduces the spirituals as historical and cultural musical sermons proclaimed in the midst of death as a key resource for exploring what it means to preach Christian hope today. The main purpose of that chapter is to utilize the spirituals and their context to argue for death as the context of preaching, reinforcing what the Ezekiel 37 passage highlights. It will conclude with some thoughts on why remembering the spirituals is important for preaching.

Following the first chapter's emphasis on the context of death, chapter 2 will demonstrate the Spirit's role in this particular understanding of preaching by using the lens of Ezekiel 37, followed by a discussion of the meaning of "spirituals" as songs of the Spirit that voice ideas of death and hope as expressions of the Spirit in these musical sermons. I will explore the interaction between the concepts of death, hope, and the Spirit by doing textual and acoustical analysis of the spirituals. These *spiritual* expressions will be shown to be significant for preaching because it is the Spirit that speaks of death and encounters death head on as part of a hope-filled sermonic discourse. This chapter will make clear that it is the Spirit who animates hope while embracing death.

Chapter 3 will be a further investigation into the nature of Christian hope and its relationship to death and the Spirit in conversation with various biblical and theological thinkers. The ideas discussed will be put into conversation with the spirituals to deepen even further what has been discovered in the spirituals for preaching. A particular stress in this chapter will be on how hope is generated through preaching in the Spirit.

Chapter 4 will be the most practical segment by providing hermeneutical approaches to reading Scripture in order to preach Christian hope and death more faithfully and effectively. This will be done by drawing on the hermeneutic of hope embedded in the spirituals. As the spirituals take the Bible as a critical resource for their musical sermonic work, this chapter takes the Bible seriously as an important partner in preaching, though it is not the only component of the homiletical arsenal.[68]

Through this particular approach to this topic of preaching, death, and hope, I desire to promote the depth of the gospel, so deep that one realizes that engaging the pit of death allows one to rise to the height of life. As Witvliet declares, "We give our people the most satisfying spiritual food not when we withhold the depth of the gospel but when we deliver it. No saccharine substitute will suffice."[69] This book aims to give a nutritious taste of the gospel truth for preaching. No easy and glamorous prosperity gospel will do. It will take death, even the hope of the death of Death. The view in the middle of the valley may not be sweet but it will be honest and uncover the tremendous need of contemporary preaching to be brutally truthful about the whole gospel, in its gory glory. To remember that we are dying "little deaths" may help us in living, hoping, and preaching.

Dry Bones

Death as the Context of Preaching

*. . . it was full of bones . . . there were very many lying in the valley,
and they were very dry.*

—EZEK. 37:1-2

Death is gwineter lay his cold icy hands on me.

—TRADITIONAL

Throughout the United States, many church buildings are surrounded by cemeteries like the Princeton Cemetery, suggesting that the church engages in a ministry of life and death. Entertaining self-help sermons or purely prosperity-gospel proclamations are insufficient when dealing with such weighty matters. One needs sermons fueled and powered by the Holy Spirit to create life and destroy death. Moreover, that image of congregations in the midst of cemeteries reveals that the preaching of the gospel occurs among the dead, in the midst of death. In many ways, Death surrounds the church, attempting to intimidate it.

Death may be successful at times, causing sermons to die before they even reach the ears and hearts of the listeners due to the fear of preachers. However, reimagining preaching through the lens of Ezekiel and the valley of dry bones may help preachers face death with more courage, just like those musical sermons, the African American spirituals.[1]

Ezekiel and the Domain of Death

Ezekiel and the valley of dry bones as the operating metaphor in this work reveals the pervasiveness of death in the preaching vocation. The historical backdrop of Ezekiel 37 is a situation of crisis for the "whole house of Israel" (v. 11). It is a collective crisis and death. Israel was already struggling in its relationship with God by defiling the temple and ignoring the holy nature of God's sanctuary, causing God to call them a "whore" (Ezek. 9). It is clear that "there was no honeymoon period" between God and Israel.[2] Eventually, the glory of God is removed from Jerusalem (Ezek. 10), indicating the correlation between the death of Israel, which is pronounced in this passage, and the absence of God. This gives God good reason to command Ezekiel to utter a diatribe and denounce the actions of Israel (Ezek. 1–24). If this is not enough despair, we hear from a Jewish fugitive that the city of Jerusalem has fallen (Ezek. 33:21), pointing to the historical fact that in 587 BCE, the city of Jerusalem, the cultural, religious, and economic center of Jewish life, fell to King Nebuchadnezzar. Israel is in a multifaceted exile and thus it is no surprise that they say "our hope is lost" (37:11). Their dreams are "dashed by Babylonian brutality."[3]

Yet, Ezekiel is called upon to "prophesy to these bones" (Ezek. 37:4), to proclaim a life-giving word to this community. It is important to realize that Ezekiel 37:1-14 is a part of the restoration discourses in this book, which reveal that "trouble don't last always" for the people of Israel. In fact, this passage points to the full-blown restoration of Israel's relationship with God in chapters 40–48 where there is a new temple and polity, and the diasporan Jews return to their land while the divine presence returns to the inner sanctuary of the temple. Indeed, the Jewish "clan, king, and cult would one day be revived."[4] This suggests an eventual holistic revival of Israel's cultural and familial relationships, political and institutional structures, and religious systems. But this future hope is not the starting point of this vision.

This is Ezekiel's third vision because "the hand of the LORD came upon" him (37:1), as it does with his other vision reports. The lifelessness and hopelessness of Israel is described with stark imagery. "The spirit of the LORD" (37:1) brings him to the valley of bones though it was believed that one could be contaminated by coming into contact with the dead (Num. 19:16-18; 2 Kgs. 23:14, 16; Ezek. 39:15-16). The spirit of the Lord brings him to the domain of death to preach. The spirit of the Lord did not give him a bigger car, bigger house, fancier jewelry, top-notch technological gadgets, more Facebook friends, or a better whoop than the winsome preacher down the block. The spirit of the Lord leads him to a "preach-off" with Death. Tom Long notes that there is "the other preacher at a funeral: Death."[5] But one does not have to go to a funeral to face death. Death is a part of life. Death is snooping around looking for its next victim, looking for ways to contaminate our existence with "little deaths." Thus every time one enters the pulpit, the preacher squares off against death, surrounded by death. Even a quick reading of this text reveals that the most prominent image is the bones, which express physical and spiritual debility (Isa. 66:14; Job 21:24). The bones are described as "very many" and "dry" (v. 2), suggesting the vast experience of death by this entire "slain" people (v. 9). "The valley of dry bones is the quintessential vision of human disaster . . ."[6] Israel is indeed dried up and dead, which is why the "graves" image is used to depict their situation when the vision is explained (vv. 12, 13). If preachers are honest, our ministries take place at ecclesial graveyards because many of us are preaching in a valley of dry bones. Ezekiel demonstrates that to preach in the Spirit means to preach in the middle of death where there are very many dry bones.

Spirituals as Musical Sermons

Creation of the Spirituals

The social context of the spirituals confirms Ezekiel's vision, but before investigating the specifics of that context, it is important to establish the spirituals as musical sermons, as preaching in their own right. Early accounts of the creation of the spirituals unveil their origin within the preaching event. One ex-slave says:

> Us ole heads used ter make them on the spurn of de moment, after we wressle with the Spirit and come thoo. But the tunes was brung from Africa by our granddaddies. Dey was jis 'miliar song . . . they calls 'em spirituals, case de Holy Spirit done revealed 'em to 'em. Some say Moss Jesus taught 'em, and I's seed 'em start in meeting. We'd all be

at the prayer house de Lord's Day, and de white preacher he'd splain the word and read whar Ezekiel done say—Dry bones gwine ter lib again. And honey, de Lord would come a-shining thoo them pages and revive dis ole nigger's heart, and I'd jump up dar and den and holler and shout and sing and pat, and dey would all cotch de words . . . and dey's all take it up and keep at it, and keep a-adding to it and den it would be a spiritual.[7]

In this case, the preacher's presentation of a biblical text provokes the individual's initial musical creation that the community then takes up as they "keep at it, and keep a-adding to it," leading to the spiritual. In his study on the chanted sermon, Jon Michael Spencer affirms this:

A perspicuous correlation exists between black preaching and the antebellum spiritual, for it is most probable that a substantial quantum of spirituals evolved via the preaching event of black worship. Although it is likely that, apart from worship, slave preachers worked at composing pleasing combinations of tune and text to later teach their spirituals to their congregations, it is probable that the more frequent development was from extemporaneous sermonizing which crescendoed *poco a poco* to intoned utterance. This melodious declamation, delineated into quasi-metrical phrases with formulaic cadence, was customarily enhanced by intervening tonal response from the congregation. Responsorial iteration of catchy words, phrases, and sentences resulted in the burgeoning of song, to which new verses could be contemporaneously adjoined. Spirituals created in such a manner were sometimes evanescent, while favorable creations were remembered and perpetuated through oral transmission.[8]

The creation of the spirituals through the extemporaneous musical sermonic delivery of preachers in conjunction with the congregational responses was apparently a common feature. Through the call and response of preacher and congregation, a song arose that I would argue is itself sermonic; musicologist Eileen Southern names this class of spirituals "the homiletic spirituals."[9] Other accounts suggest that the spiritual originated when a song leader was so moved by a preacher's sermon that he or she interrupted the sermon by answering him with a song.[10] Nonetheless, the spiritual was rooted in the preaching moment.

Many scholars take it a step further by even asserting, as Spencer does above, that slave preachers were probably the main creators and teachers of the spirituals. At least there is a "strong suspicion" that this is so.[11] James

Weldon Johnson, an early interpreter of the spirituals, refers respectfully to the creator of the spirituals as the "black and unknown bards" and does not equate the creators with preachers per se. Rather, he claims that the makers and leaders of song were a "recognized order of bards" who possessed "a gift of melody, a talent for poetry, a strong voice, and a good memory."[12] Despite this difference of opinion on the creator and teacher of these songs, there is agreement on the connection between the creation of the spirituals and preaching, though spirituals were also created apart from communal worship. Moreover, in his collection of poetry written in the manner of old-time folk sermons, *God's Trombones*, Johnson reveals the natural overlap of preaching and spirituals when he describes his work and declares, "I have, naturally, felt the influence of the Spirituals,"[13] though it was impossible to create the actual atmosphere that he experienced. He says that his sermonic poems would be best intoned because "the undertone of singing was often soft accompaniment to parts of the sermon."[14] John Work calls this musical accompaniment the "moan."[15]

Others go beyond viewing the spirituals as mere accompaniment to the sermon. E. Franklin Frazier notes that slave "preaching consisted of singing sacred songs which have come to be known as the Spirituals."[16] Thus the spirituals were not only created in the preaching moment sparked by preachers' musicality and congregational "talk back" or sung to "add momentum to the gospel"[17] in its accompaniment, but the very nature of preaching "consisted of" singing these songs. Singing the spirituals was a part of what it meant to preach; thus even singing the spirituals counted as preaching. The spirituals were the word set to music and their composition by a preacher during a sermon has led some to call these types "preaching spirituals."[18] John Lovell asserts that "Many spirituals could qualify as sermons."[19] These songs were indeed "prayers, praises, and sermons."[20] All of this suggests a convergence between the singing of spirituals and preaching. The most profound sign of their union is the musicality of both.

Musical Nature

One of the key traits of the spirituals as sermons is their musical essence. African American sermons have historically been known to be musical because music and speech are inseparable as African traditions treat songs like speech and speech like songs. Henry Mitchell reminds us that the "languages of Africa are manifestly tonal."[21] There is a "proneness to sing" revealing "[their] natural self, which is a musical self."[22] This musical self is poignantly revealed in what is known as the chanted sermon. According to Bruce Rosenberg, "the chanted folk sermon is never far from the spiritual"; he views the chanted sermon as a "conflation of the prose sermon and the spiritual."[23] Their historical roots come out of the same soil. In fact, chanting preachers know themselves to be "spiritual" preachers as opposed to "manuscript" preachers.[24] This has to do with whether one uses a manuscript or not to assist in preaching, but it also suggests the equation of "spiritual" with a musical type of preaching, known as chanting, intoning, or whooping. The climax of a sermon that shifts to chanting is described in a 1932 essay: "With the coming of the spirit . . . the speaker's entire demeanor changes. . . . His voice, changed in pitch, takes on a mournful, singing quality, and words flow from his lips in such a manner as to make an understanding of them almost impossible.[25] This "singing quality" of the sermon is known as "giving gravey."[26] It is a *spiritual* way of preaching that is tonal and "sonorous," making a sermon melodious.[27] Thus the sermon sings and this is "spiritual" preaching. The chanted portion of a sermon is the most obvious convergence of song and speech, revealing that "preaching is musical."[28] In addition, though the most popular opinion is that the spirituals originated from the preaching moment, Rosenberg writes, "One is inclined to approach the origin of the chanted sermon by the circuitous route of the spiritual for several reasons. The sermons are repetitious in the same ways the spirituals are. And an extraordinary number of sermon lines come directly from spirituals."[29] From his perspective, the chanted sermon stems from the spirituals, which may be another reason for calling it "spiritual" preaching.

Regardless of the debates on the origins of the sermon and spirituals, there is a symbiosis between singing and preaching, particularly the singing of the spirituals and the intonation of sermons. This symbiotic relationship is demonstrated in numerous ways, including, but not limited to, performative dimensions, such as the "African call-and-response song style,"[30] which is present in both singing and preaching. This convergence prompts Valentino Lassiter to assert, "The slave preacher . . . worked much in the same mode as the singer of spirituals."[31] The cultural tradition of overlap between singing and preaching, song and speech, continues today. The "musical voice" of old-time black preachers, the voice of a trombone, permeates various contemporary African American preaching traditions.[32] Preachers may quote hymns or spirituals in their sermons, but they will also sing. Singers will also preach. Queen of gospel music and pastor Shirley Caesar captures in her own ministry the fusion of singing and preaching in an interview when she says, "I sing my sermons and I preach my songs."[33] Singing and preaching are different sides of the same homiletical coin.

Contemporary theorists of preaching affirm that singing is preaching and preaching is singing. One of the key homileticians to highlight the musicality of black preaching is William C. Turner. He writes poetically that during the climactic surplus of the sermon, the preacher becomes "an instrument—a flute through which divine air is blown, a harp whose strings are plucked by God."[34] This description is rightly musical as the preacher uses music to do the ministry of proclamation. Elsewhere, he calls the music of preaching "singing in the spirit."[35] In *The Jazz of Preaching*, Kirk Byron Jones also affirms the marriage between music and preaching when he writes, "Musicians play notes; preachers play words. Sometimes they even sing them."[36] In his eulogy for pastor Sandy Ray, Gardner Taylor noted that it was difficult to determine whether in Ray's preaching one "heard music half-spoken or speech half-sung."[37] This rich interplay of sung speech and spoken song has deep roots in the historical relationship between the spirituals and preaching. It is a continuous trend in many black homiletical traditions because music in many ways has been as natural as breathing. As noted earlier, for those culturally rooted in Africa, the musical self is the natural self, thus sermons that sing and songs that preach are religiously natural. Musicality as a common characteristic of black preaching fuses the spirituals to preaching and helps one begin to recognize the spirituals as sermons, too, sermons that can teach us about preaching today. However, the emerging parallels between singing the spirituals and preaching do not only consist of the obvious musical nature but the ways in which biblical texts are linked to contextual realities.

(Con)Textual Nature

Another reason to claim the spirituals as sermons and as a helpful resource is the way they appropriate the Bible in a manner that speaks to concrete realities in life, conversing with both text and context. The strong parallels between the sermon and the spiritual include the following: "narrative technique, the picturesqueness and the concreteness, the emphasis on personal characteristics, the familiarity with the deity . . ."[38] A part of the narrative technique is how the preacher tells the story of God to the people of God. Telling the story has been critical in African American preaching; Henry Louis Gates even claims "only black music-making was as important to the culture of African-Americans as has been the fine art of storytelling."[39] Gates puts music on par with story and W. E. B. Du Bois asserts them as the same gift, a "gift of story and song."[40] A song tells a story, too, just like preaching. The spirituals are "story theology."[41] They proclaim a story of how black people came over a way that had been drenched by tears and blood. They reveal how those under harsh existential circumstances "got over." The spiritual "You May Have All Dis World, But Give Me Jesus" represented the "narcotic doctrine" that the folk preacher instilled in those suffering under Pharaoh's hand in slavery.[42] The narrative messages, the stories, of the preacher and the spirituals were the same. They worked hand in hand as companions. The spirituals even "helped to shape and to tenor the message of the slave preacher."[43] The message was the same as singer and preacher told the story. Their hermeneutical lenses were similar, especially as they interpreted the Bible to help tell the story.

An important aspect of preaching is engaging the Bible as an aid to proclaiming the gospel. "Exegesis of the text" is critical for proclamation.[44] The spirituals are no different in that they engage the Bible to help tell their story while they preach. Howard Thurman names the Bible as a key source for the spirituals. He says, "The Christian Bible furnished much of the imagery and ideas with which the slave singers fashioned their melodies."[45] A brief survey of spiritual titles reveals the importance of Scripture in the spirituals: "Joshua Fit the Battle of Jericho," "Go Down, Moses," "Didn't My Lord Deliver Daniel?," "Mary Had a Baby, Yes, Lord," "We Are Climbing Jacob's Ladder," or "Were You There When They Crucified My Lord?" Singing and preaching were significant means for conveying the story of the Bible. "Through the sermon, as well as spirituals and gospel songs, the Jewish and Christian Scriptures entered and shaped the imaginative world of African-Americans."[46]

The spirituals, like hymns, function as midrashim. According to Tom Troeger, hymns are midrashic because "hymn writers combine the spirit and concerns of their culture with the resonance and depth of the ancient text."[47] The spirituals operate in the same way as they merge the concerns of the enslaved with the biblical story. For example, the spiritual, "Didn't My Lord Deliver Daniel?," says, "Didn't my Lord deliver Daniel, deliver Daniel, deliver Daniel, Didn't my Lord deliver Daniel, an' why not-a every man." They needed deliverance and this story spoke to their situation of oppression. Especially when it comes to the story of Jesus, the spirituals fuse into his story "their very own pathos."[48]

Dey crucified my Lord, an' he never said a mumblin' word.
Dey crucified my Lord, an' he never said a mumblin' word,
Not a word—not a word—not a word.

Dey nailed Him to de tree, an' he never said a mumblin' word.
Dey nailed Him to de tree, an' he never said a mumblin' word.
Not a word—not a word—not a word.

The piercing, blood flowing, and the eventual dying of Jesus in the Bible are their story. The spirituals reveal the Bible as a mirror of our existence to help tell the story, the good news in our concrete situation. However, if the spirituals only engaged the Bible, a text, they would not be sermons because preaching is not a mere reiteration of the text or pure exposition of a biblical text. Preaching as exemplified in the spirituals must also speak to particular contextual realities. Sermons should relate the Bible to life, interpreting Scripture in light of one's *Sitz im Leben* (life situation). In other words, preachers should also do an "exegesis of the situation."[49] The spirituals do this by relating the text, the Bible in this case, to context.

One man tells how these songs were created in light of particular experiences of the slave. He says, "I'll tell you; it's dis way. My master call me up and order me a short peck of corn and a hundred lash. My friends see it and is sorry for me. When dey come to de praise meeting dat night dey sing about it. Some's very good singers and know how; and dey work it in, work it in, you know; till dey get it right; and dat's de way."[50] In this case, the spirituals created relate to the happenings of the day. They speak to the local experience of slaves as an attempt to minister to the surrounding needs of the community. The needs of a community should shape the sermon. Thurman says the slaves had "deep needs"[51] and the spirituals were a sermonic attempt to meet those needs, regardless of the situation. These songs were sung at work and leisure, to children, over the sick and dead, at praise meetings, and in other situations. "The very heart beats of life" were expressed through these songs.[52] These songs transferred from location to location and generation to generation, causing changes to songs and even sometimes to their interpretation based on the setting, dialect, and occasion. These songs were flexibly suited to the life in which they were sung as the soul of a people was expressed in the language of the people, the "mother tongue of the Spirit."[53] The vernacular articulation of the word is important for contextually sensitive preaching. The spirituals as folk songs, the sermons of a collective group, are the "painted picture of a soul" in the "colors of music."[54] This soul-full music, this *spiritual* preaching, like typical sermons, is focused on the survival of a people, thus they pay close attention to the needs of the community. The soul that is voiced is communal, which suggests another key trait of the spirituals as musical sermons.

Communal Nature

The spirituals, just like preaching, are not the sole property of one individual but represent the collective voice of a people. Preaching is a communal word. The preacher goes "to the pulpit from the pew,"[55] revealing that the preacher is part of a larger community. The same is true for the spirituals. Dale Andrews notes, "The community participation common to black preaching has also produced similar worship traditions in black spirituals."[56] In both, there is a rich sense of communal participation or what Evans Crawford calls "participant proclamation."[57] Most obvious in this cultural tradition is the performance of the call and response between leader and community, as noted earlier. For instance, in the spiritual "Go Down, Moses," as a leader sings, "Thus saith the Lord, bold Moses said," the community responds, "Let my people go." The call and response continues until everyone joins in on the refrain,

> Go down, Moses,
> 'Way down in Egypt land,
> Tell ole Pharaoh,
> Let my people go.

Furthermore, what accentuates the communal nature of the spirituals as sermons is their unknown character, in terms of authorship and time and place of origin. In his poem to honor the creator of the spirituals, "O Black and Unknown Bards," Johnson stresses that the bards are "forgot, unfamed, . . . untaught, unknown, unnamed . . ."[58] There are no specifics about who specifically created the spirituals. This suggests that these musical sermons belong to the community and not any one individual. They are "unnamed" because the community trumps the individual in this case. The unknown character of these songs implies that they are communal musical sermons. Even if most spirituals were created by talented individuals, as some scholars suggest,[59] the community provides the dominant themes as these songs are passed along and altered from one generation to the next via oral transmission. Also, the spirituals were "originally intended only for group singing" because "Negro spirituals are not solo or quartette material."[60] These spirituals are "owned" by the entire community.

These are trademarks of folk music. As these songs travel across time, they reveal a type of consensus within a community regarding beliefs, patterns of behavior, and so forth. Lovell notes that "in folk music, the individual invents; the community selects. The racial character of a song, therefore, is due to communal choice, not communal invention." Folk songs, just like folk sermons, "grow straight out of the needs of the people."[61] The folks matter in preaching and, particularly with a musical sense of preaching, music in African culture is about "the bond of fellowship" between humanity.[62] People sing or preach with each other and not for one another. The spirituals, like preaching, are "folk art" and the preacher is a "folk artist" or a "recondite folksinger" who engages in "folk work."[63] The "folk" focus means that the spirituals as sermons are in tune with the local community and its needs to such an extent that these sermons are collective property. Musical sermons arise out of the communal heart. This collective heart was under attack in the particular context out of which the spirituals arose, revealing how death is a context of preaching.

Social Context of the Spirituals

The spirituals, musical sermons, were forged in the flame of slavery, where the stench of death permeated life. These songs were literally a matter of life and death. James Cone reminds us that "No theological interpretation of the black spirituals can be valid that ignores the cultural environment that created them. The black experience in America is a history of servitude and resistance, of survival *in the land of death*. It is the story of black life in chains and of what that meant for the souls and bodies of black people."[64] This death-dealing environment is the root of black preaching and singing. It is the foundation of African American religiosity, "a path through the blood of the slaughtered."[65] Africans were stolen from their motherland to take "a treacherous, transatlantic journey of terror"[66] called the Middle Passage to the mainland of the Americas, a supposed land of the free. But "Before the ships sailed, many leaped overboard and drowned rather than be enslaved. African women, heavy with child, plunged sharpened bamboo sticks into their bellies to kill the unborn rather than have it be born a slave. Many refused to eat or drink and sank into melancholia so deep they died on board. We never did like being slaves!"[67] This is why the spiritual rang out, "Oh freedom, oh freedom, oh freedom all over me, an' before I'd be a slave, I'd be buried in my grave, an' go home to ma Lawd an' be free." This context of suffering was "the fires of purgatory."[68] Some were even literally burned and tortured to death on lynching trees as if they were not even human. The enslaved had every right to sing, "Nobody knows the trouble I see, nobody knows but Jesus . . ."

The sorrow and grief were overwhelming due to the existential reality of brutality. Yet, Johnson insightfully declares, "It is strange!" that from these people enduring such harsh realities this "noble music sprang." He attempts to paint a fuller picture of the sinful situation when he writes, "they were, suddenly cut off from the moorings of their native culture, scattered without regard to their old tribal relations, having to adjust themselves to a completely alien civilization, having to learn a strange language, and, moreover, held under an increasingly harsh system of slavery."[69] In other words, the spirituals rose out of a situation not only of physical death but of "social death."[70] Separated from what was familiar, even family, the spiritual "Sometimes I feel like a motherless child" was created. Thurman says:

> For the slave, freedom was not on the horizon; there stretched ahead the long road down which there marched in interminable lines only the rows of cotton, the sizzling heat, the riding overseer with his rawhide whip, the auction block where families were torn asunder, the barking of the bloodhounds—all this, but not freedom.

> Human slavery has been greatly romanticized by the illusion of distance, the mint julep, the long Southern twilight, and the lazy sweetness of blooming magnolias. But it must be intimately remembered that slavery was a dirty, sordid, inhuman business. When the slaves were taken from their homeland, the primary social unit was destroyed, and all immediate tribal and family ties were ruthlessly broken. This meant the severing of the link that gave the individual African a sense of *persona*. There is no more hapless victim than one who is cut off from family, from language, from one's roots.[71]

The slave's persona was under attack not only through severed relational ties but by the "all-out assault on the black body."[72] Oppression seeks to destroy one's humanity, yet these musical sermons were proclaimed by those whose humanity was under attack. A context of death could not mute this life-giving music, even a death perpetuated by fellow Christians who practiced Christianity in a cruel manner.

Despite the failings of the church to act Christian, the enslaved contin-ued to sing and proclaim, "I'm a rollin', I'm a rollin', I'm a rollin' through an unfriendly worl' . . ." The world was unfriendly but so was the church, yet blacks kept rolling along and pushing forward in life despite the vast experiences of death, the very many dry bones in their valley. Though they were snatched from Africa, they did not lose their song. They sang in a strange land, in exile, because their music was portable. In fact, the con-text of death, like Ezekiel's valley of dry bones, provided a distinct texture for these sermons. "Slavery . . . gave color to [their] music. Slavery was the starting point and Heaven was the goal of [their] life."[73] As with these songs, black preaching begins in suffering, pain, and death. It is the start-ing point for the vital preaching of Christian hope. This is not to celebrate death and slavery but it is to acknowledge it as the social setting of the spirituals, musical sermons that have much to teach contemporary preach-ers. As in our day, there was then the "tragedy of great need."[74] Human need is no respecter of persons as many face "little deaths" on a daily basis. But what these spirituals also reveal is a profound way to respond to one's situation of death.

Spirituals as a Response to Death

A Singing Soul

The spirituals as musical sermons reveal that preaching is a critical response to a domain of death. Ezekiel, when in the domain of death, was called to "prophesy to the bones," to say a word. He could have been asked to do a wide variety of things in response to pervasive death, yet God called Ezekiel to preach as a response to death. Words have power and melodious words perhaps even more. To sing a sermon in order to counter death was natural for those whose "soul is a song" and whose life "a life of song."[75] Music was not just the soul of the civil rights movement in the United States, it was and is the soul of black folks. Du Bois presents this notion implicitly by using epigraphic musical refrains of the spirituals at the beginning of each chapter in *The Soul of Black Folks*.[76] The heart of the soul of black folks is a song, the spiritual specifically.

The black soul sang through death and until death. They possessed a "gift of story and song" in an "ill-harmonized and unmelodious land."[77] They brought sweet melodies to a land that attempted to kill their song because their soul was a singer. They endured great suffering but not without a song, which is why James Cone has declared, *"Black history is a spiritual!"*[78] The spiritual was their soul and it represented what it meant to be human, even as they were dehumanized. These particular songs of the soul have become not solely black songs but are human songs that are a "multipurposed anthem of the human spirit."[79] Those who were deemed subhuman were teachers of humanity through the spirituals as they sang in response to their harsh situation. As long as they sang, there was still hope. The words of the poet Paul Dunbar ring true for the enslaved: "I sing my song and all is well."[80] All is well because the spirituals were not just songs of the soul; they were life itself.

Song as Life

To sing was to live. The setting of death could not mute the life-giving spirituals. Singing was a vital response to death because by doing so the enslaved were countering death with life. The spirituals might have been considered "sorrow songs"[81] by some, but they were still songs that meant life continued to pulse in their oppressed veins. Some scholars say, "Without songs to sing, life would be diminished."[82] For the slave, however, without a song, life would be destroyed by death because through the spiritual, a musical sermon, the enslaved "chants new life."[83] This is the heart of preaching—chanting new life in the midst of death. The "urge to sing" the spirituals was just as indispensable to living as breath flowing through the body.[84] "The balm in Gilead was the spiritual itself."[85] The actual phenomenon of singing was life giving and a means of survival.

Musical preaching via the spirituals was essential for survival in the valley of the dry bones of slavery. To imagine black religiosity without them is impossible because they are the soul of a people fighting to survive. These musical sermons enabled survival because they "cut a path through the wilderness of despair."[86] Melodies paved a path toward freedom. Bernice Johnson Reagon, civil-rights singer and activist, argues that the "Spirituals were songs created as leverage, as salve, as voice, as a bridge over troubles one could not endure without the flight of song and singing."[87] Without these spiritual melodies from heaven, many African Americans would not have survived. If they wanted to live, they had to sing, they had to preach musically.

These songs provided strength to the singing preachers. Former slave Vinnie Brunson said that singing "wuz des de way [the slave] 'spressed his feelin's an hit made him relieved."[88] It helped them endure the hardships of life. But this is not surprising because "whenever human beings are caught in oppressive suffering, songs emerge."[89] Musical sermons give strength to the weak and weary, battered and bruised. They are not a laughing matter. These songs are nothing short of a "miracle."[90] Many chose to sing and not sulk. This "is one of those psychic phenomena which show the inscrutable workings of the Creator."[91] Even today, signs of the Creator are present through songs in the domain of death. During the aftermath of the 2010 earthquake in Haiti, there was a lot of singing even while there was much crying, screaming, moaning, and groaning. Singing is not the expected response to catastrophe. In one case, Ena Zizi, a seventy-year-old woman, had been buried for a week in earthquake rubble that was at least three stories high from the ground. When she was pulled out of the rubble, she was seriously dehydrated and had a broken leg and a dislocated hip. But that did not stop her; rather, Ena began to sing. Her body was worn and her throat was weary but life was singing.[92] Her song in the rubble, as with the spirituals, was "a complete and final refusal to be stopped."[93] That song was a sound of the "glad defiance"[94] of life bubbling up. But she was not alone as others sang on the streets day and night. The songs that rose from the rubble of this catastrophe were deeply communal for the life of a people.

Singing in Community (Secretly)

As blacks responded to the context of death with musical sermons historically, the soul singing of life had a collective heartbeat. An entire community responded to death head-on with musical courage. In terms of music making, it is rare for the African to play for another; rather, he or she plays or sings *with* someone else. "The great lesson of African music is human brotherhood."[95] It is a bond in which anyone can sing. The "unknown" quality of the spirituals suggests that they are "the spirit of the people struggling to be free."[96] What is voiced is the communal voice, a community hymn sing that fights for life, the life of a community. Riggins Earl writes, "The singing act itself symbolized the socially objectified consciousness of the oppressed."[97] These songs created a sense of community, a social body that coalesced for the cause of liberation. Singing reaffirmed a common bond and reduced social alienation and feelings of a social death. The children of Israel struggled to sing a song in a strange land, but African Americans had to sing because "their *being* depended upon a song."[98] Singing solidified the community even if they had to sing in secret.

Many of the musical sermons were preached in what is called the "invisible institution." Eugene Genovese writes, "The slaves' religious meetings would be held in secret when their masters forbade all such; or when their masters forbade all except Sunday meetings; or when rumors of rebellion or disaffection led even indulgent masters to forbid them so as to protect the people from trigger-happy patrollers; or when the slaves wanted to make sure that no white would hear them."[99] These secret sessions gave a sense of communal autonomy and strength. This gathering empowered the enslaved to endure and even resist their unjust oppression. This "institution" and other independent places of worship developed by the old-time preachers are important to highlight because "except for these separate places of worship there never would have been any Spirituals."[100] This strong statement reveals that the spiritual implies a community, one that celebrates and laments in the face of death. This kind of community that performs a musical sermonic "collective exorcism"[101] of the demonic powers of slavery is an obvious threat to those in power.

Singing as Resistance

Fear of Insurrection. The presence of a singing, preaching, and worshiping community can be viewed as a threat to those in power. The spirituals sung in community spread fear among the oppressors, especially after numerous rebellions. Genovese notes,

> Although blacks preached with some ease during the eighteenth century, they were severely curbed during the nineteenth. Each insurrectionary scare from Gabriel's to Vesey's to Nat Turner's led to a wave of repression. Especially after 1831, laws forbade free Negroes to preach to slaves or sought to register and control them or required whites to be present when any black man preached. But the preachers, free and slave, carried on.[102]

Those in power saw the gathered community as an impetus toward insurrection. Singing and preaching, especially in the secret "hush harbors," were viewed as "a threat to the social order"[103] and potential cover for insurrection plotting. To preach, sing, or pray, even at home, was hazardous to the slave. If found engaging in these activities, they could be beaten or flogged or, worse, killed. There are numerous accounts of this lockdown on worship. One report declares, "My Bos didn' 'low us to go to church,

er to pray er sing. Iffen he ketched us prayin 'er singin' he whupped us."[104]
Despite the forces of death literally beating down on them, the slaves "carried on" with their practices many times. Faith and courage could not be whipped out of them. One slave said, "When I was a slave my master would sometimes whip me *awful*, specially when he knew I was praying. He was determined to whip the Spirit out of me, but he could never do it, for de more he whip the more the Spirit make me *content* to be whipt."[105] The fear of whites was so overwhelming that they were even skeptical of slave funerals. Singing and preaching in any venue were a to threat the powers of death because "you cannot sing a song and not change your condition."[106] These practices were a form of resistance to death, both blatant and subtle.

Blatant Opposition. Much scholarship has given attention to the more subtle resistance of the spirituals through their double coded meanings, which I discuss below; however, there are open signs of resistance to deathly circumstances in many of the spirituals. In his narrative *My Bondage and My Freedom*, Frederick Douglass says this about the spirituals: "Every tone was a testimony against slavery, and a prayer to God for deliverance from chains."[107] The spirituals were "fatal words of confrontation and conflict."[108] Those that claim docility was the entire story miss the explicit resistance to slavery and white oppression. For instance, the following spiritual is forthright about its resistance with the repetition of "no more":

> No more auction block for me, No more, No more, No more auction block for me, many thousand gone. No more peck o'corn for me, No more, no more, No more peck o'corn for me, many thousand gone. No more driver's lash for me. . . . No more pint o'salt for me. . . . No more hundred lash for me. . . . No more mistress' call for me. . .

The enslaved wanted "no more" death from anyone. They wanted freedom so much that death was sometimes more preferable than life. One must remember that "Black resistance has roots stretching back to the slave ships, the auction blocks, and the plantation regime. It began when the first black person decided that death would be preferable to slavery."[109] The enslaved sang about it, too. "Before I'd be a slave, I'd be buried in my grave an' go home to my Lawd an' be free." Yearning for death was a form of resistance against the life they endured and they knew that "Everybody talkin' 'bout heab'n ain't goin' dere."

Subtle Opposition. However, their musical forms of opposition were not always blatant. It was subtle, too. The enslaved performed a "pantomime of survival—smiling when they wanted to weep, laughing when they boiled with anger, feigning ignorance when they brimmed with intelligence."[110] One of the masterful components of the spirituals is their double or coded meaning or what has been called a "mask," a prominent characteristic in African music. According to Lovell, "the mask was for protection against whites; the secrecy was for binding the slaves together through messages of assurance."[111] The use of mask and symbol, double entendre, was a form of lyrical resistance to the context of death. It is a secret protest against pain, thus many spirituals should not be read literally. Wearing the mask requires figurative interpretation. The singing of spirituals is covert communication in a theo-musical, theo-poetic manner. For instance, one can read the spiritual "Lord, I Want to Be a Christian in-a My Heart" as a critique of the "surface operator" slave-master Christian type: the slave desires true religion "in-a my heart" as opposed to the surface external expression of Christianity they see their oppressors demonstrating.[112] One may assume it is just an expression of piety, but understanding the coded nature of these songs suggests that it can also be a protest of the kind of Christian witness they observe. "Go Down, Moses," quoted above, is another example of the mask. On the surface, one may hear its refrain as only a reiteration of the Bible story about the children of Israel enslaved in Egypt. But if one understands the mask worn by these musical sermons, one can hear the subtextual parallel of the slaves' yearning for a Moses to be sent into their Egyptian land of slavery in order to deliver them from the pharaohs of slaveocracy and declare, "Let my people go." The enslaved were Israel; Egypt was the bondage of earthly slavery; Pharaoh was the oppressors.

Spirituals such as these were secret modes of communication that only the black community understood. They were musical indictments against their oppression. They signified resistance. Other spirituals like "Steal Away," "There's a Great Camp Meeting," "Walk Together Children Don't Get Weary," and "Wade in the Water" were hidden ways of announcing events, like a local news report that is only understood by those who speak the same language. Douglass is explicit about the double meaning in the spirituals:

> A keen observer might have detected in our repeated singing of
> 'O Canaan, sweet Canaan, I am bound for the land of Canaan,'

something more than a hope of reaching heaven. We meant to reach the north—and the north was our Canaan.

> In the lips of some, it meant the expectation of a speedy summons to a world of spirits; but in the lips of our company, it simply meant a speedy pilgrimage toward a free state, and deliverance from all the evils and dangers of slavery.[113]

These songs were not mere melodies of heaven but tunes of earth.

Whether the language was the "kingdom," "heaven," "Canaan land," the "promised land" or "over Jordan," there could be a dual meaning in light of the "mask" ideal. Revisionist history argues that the notion of heaven in these musical sermons is "a principle of social criticism well camouflaged in the prominent Christian language of the day. Most important, this revised interpretation claims that the African slaves discerned the symbol heaven as an implicit criticism of everything in the society that maintained slavery and racial oppression."[114] "Heaven" and related terms were not an otherworldly haven but this-worldly linguistic modes of resistance to death. John Blassingame asserts, "As other-worldly as they often appear, the spirituals served as much more than opiates and escapist fantasies. They affirmed the slave's personal autonomy and recognized the reality of his earthly suffering. While looking beyond the dismal present to a brighter future, the spiritual enabled blacks to transcend degradation and to find the emotional security to endure pain."[115] These songs resisted dehumanization and demonization and grabbed ahold of hope and the future in the face of opposition.

The spirituals were a part of "an insistent cultural antiphony"[116] to the way white oppressors operated in the world. The antiphonal response represented by the double coded spirituals continued the "tradition of indirection"[117] among preachers. The lyrics were not the sole dimension of the mask because melodies masked what was really happening in the subtextual world of defiance and resistance. The subtle form of resistance was also present in the performance of the spiritual, particularly the use of the body.

Gags were placed on slave preachers as a means to silence[118] but gags could not prevent the body from talking, rhythmically resisting oppression. Some say, "The chief vehicle for the *performance* of the Negro spiritual was the human voice,"[119] yet singing is sound moving through one's body. A cultural "somatic sensibility" converges with music especially.[120]

The historical performance of the spiritual involves the swaying of the body. Johnson describes it when he writes,

> In all authentic American Negro music the rhythms may be divided roughly into two classes—rhythms based on the swinging of head and body and rhythms based on the patting of hands and feet. Again speaking roughly, the rhythms of the Spirituals fall in the first class. . . . The 'swing' of the Spirituals is an altogether subtle and elusive thing. It is subtle and elusive because it is in perfect union with the religious ecstasy that manifests itself in the swaying bodies of a whole congregation, swaying as if responding to the baton of some extremely sensitive conductor. So it is very difficult, if not impossible, to sing these songs sitting or standing coldly still, and at the same time capture the spontaneous 'swing' which is of their very essence.[121]

The subtle "swing" was present in the clandestine gatherings even as people had to sing with a "hush" because of the restrictive laws against gathering. Melva Costen says that even the "'silent songs'" [were] expressed in kinesthetic movements and rhythms . . ."[122] The body sang as it moved, swaying even in sorrow. The ring shout is a classic example of the embodied nature of singing spirituals.[123]

The musical sermon is incomplete without some sort of body movement—dancing, swaying, rocking, tapping, clapping. The "swing" suggests another form of resistance to death. In slavery, the oppressors attempted to control the black body. But in slave religion, "the slaves would take their bodies back."[124] The sway or swing of the black bodies in the performance of the spirituals was resistance to "Black bodies swinging in the Southern breeze" on lynching trees.[125] Their sway as they sang was a counterswing to the swaying of death in their environment. This bodily swing was a way of taking control of one's space, voice, body, and life. They could swing in the face of death to resist it. They could affirm that God was present with them in their bodies. The swing of the spiritual was an affirmation of divine presence and human dignity to such an extent that bruised and beaten black bodies "became an icon of God."[126] These musical sermons revealed that they were somebody when others treated them like nobody. Their literal bodies swayed in the wind of the Spirit(ual) to counteract the bodies in the southern breeze. By doing so, they showed that they were a collective body rhythmically "swinging to the movement of life."[127] This *spiritual* hunger for life in the face of death is something to be remembered, especially for those ministering in a valley with very many dry bones.

Importance of Cultural Memory for Preaching

There is a proverb that says, "Don't forget the bridge that brought you over." The musical bridge that is the spirituals brought black peoples over troubled waters in the past and present. To forget them is to forget how many preachers arrived where they are today by standing on the shoulders of the unknown black bards. Their melodies, biblical insight, contextual sensitivity, performance practices, and sheer will to live shape the nature of preaching today. To forget them is to lose the deep *spiritual* roots of preaching. Remembering the past sheds light on the present. The past possesses rich pedagogical wisdom. The hymn declares, "We've come this far by faith," but we still have much further to go in our preaching because "every shut eye ain't sleep, every good-bye ain't gone." The door of the past cannot be closed and in the case of the spirituals, it should not be because there is further development and growth needed in our preaching. We need to keep the history of the spirituals open for contemporary knowledge, but that history, as described above, is partly brutal and inhumane.

Some want to forget slavery because "Slavery is the site of black victimage and thus of tradition's intended erasure."[128] Some are ashamed of singing the spirituals because of their connection to slavery. They are considered unsophisticated musical ditties that weaken African Americans. Those who support erasure of past slavery from historical memory will also cry that slavery was not the totality of the black experience in the past, but that there was also dignity. This is true, but the dignity was held in the midst of slavery, death. "We have come over a way that with tears has been watered."[129] To forget that wet path of tears would be a sign of disrespect to the ancestors, the "many thousand gone." To remember is to honor them.

Furthermore, I would argue that to forget slavery is actually impossible because, just like Lazarus's body, death "stinketh" (John 11:39, KJV), and the stench of death from slavery lingers in today's atmosphere. Death cannot be avoided and the spirituals demonstrate how death can be encountered courageously. This is tremendously empowering toward reimagining what preaching is because, as Toni Morrison reminds us, "the act of imagination is bound up with memory."[130] As one remembers, one reimagines, even re-members, the essence of preaching. This reimagining leads us to the place of death and contamination, the valley of dry bones.

If one does not sever ties with the human history of the spirituals, one will not only learn lessons of life, but gain homiletical wisdom that shapes a distinct perspective on the task of preaching. Remembering the spirituals provides numerous lessons for understanding preaching.

Remembering Human Tragedy

The first lesson from the spirituals that preachers can learn is that human tragedy, death, pain, and suffering are a part of human life, thus a critical component of the context for preaching. To remember the spirituals, one must remember that death and suffering are pervasive. No human being escapes "de troubles of the world." Thurman declares that "suffering stalks [humanity], never losing the scent, and soon or late seizes upon him [or her] to wreak its devastation."[131] Black preaching expressions are historically rooted in death-wielding devastation unless someone suffers from cultural amnesia and forgets this. The history of pain is part of the power of African American preaching. This is not to celebrate death and pain but to acknowledge it as part of human reality. To remember the spirituals for thinking about preaching means that one remembers a deadly, bloody, and tear-filled past in human history. As noted, "We have come over a way that with tears has been watered. We have come treading a path through the blood of the slaughtered." Tears, blood, and death, not health, wealth, and prosperity, have been the heart of the existential journey of black people in the world. "The blood of the martyrs is the seed of faith,"[132] says Raboteau, and for my homiletical purpose, the blood of the martyrs fertilizes the soil of our preaching. Black preachers stand in their blood to preach. Their blood cries out from the pulpit every time we stand to preach because they have paved the path of proclamation.

From the waters of the Middle Passage to the blood spilled in the "land of the free," from slavery to the Jim Crow era to the current burdens of today, these martyrs teach us "that suffering must be lived through; it can't be avoided by any of the spurious means of escape that people use to distract one another from real life. Life is bittersweet, joyful sadness."[133] This is what the "haunting echo"[134] of the spirituals teaches preachers. Tragedy and death are aspects of the gospel. Preaching is supposed to be a truth-telling enterprise and have a "truth orientation"[135] about it. If preaching does not acknowledge the truth of death and suffering in the world, it is a doxological lie that perpetuates homiletical dishonesty. But the honest truth is that, for many, life is bitter and sweet is sour. The historical path of human existence

has been paved with the innocent blood of people, the blood of our ancestors. African diasporan cultural memory is moist with bitter blood.

The spilling of innocent human blood reveals the vast human need in
the world. These human atrocities then and now provide a ministry opportunity for preachers. Preaching is a ministry to serve the needs of those in
its hearing. Tragedy provides a context for the human need and challenges
preaching to reclaim its function as ministry, service, to those who are
suffering in varied ways. Preaching is not just an event or a practice or an
art. It is *ministry* to those who are dying in our midst. Many people in the
pews are in an exilic experience, not knowing whether they will be delivered. Exile is no respecter of persons; however, African Americans are in
a particular predicament in the United States. Houston Baker asserts that
privileged middle-class blacks "are being told paradoxically that if we are
to be liked *as blacks*, we must not only forget the majority of those in the
United States who are, in fact, black, but also relinquish all thoughts of an
American past where the reality for the entire majority of sons and fathers
of blackness was slavery, convict lease labor, menial employment, second-
class citizenship, social death, and immobilizing poverty."[136] Forgetting
would betray human suffering and the reality of racism. Yet, one cannot
forget the past because pain is still present.

Sometimes we still feel like motherless children due to loneliness or
isolation. Little deaths with huge ramifications still pervade life—drive-
by shootings, contraction of AIDS, war, genocide, famine, cancer, family dysfunction, abuse, suffering from those who have just lost a child or
those who want children but cannot have any. One does not even need a
gun to kill someone anymore; just imprison another "minority" or traffic
another child for sex or perpetuate institutional racism. No one, regardless
of race, gender, or class, is immune from suffering or the little deaths of
life. The reality of death and suffering stares humanity in the face everyday
but some sectors of the church attempt to erase or ignore this fact of life
to such an extent that death is segregated from theological and ecclesial
discourse and action. Life-giving ministry cannot happen without dealing
with death and preaching is a ministry to those who are dying little deaths.

Just as St. Augustine's tears flowed so freely that they formed a pillow
for his heart,[137] I am suggesting that death, literally and figuratively, is the
pillow, the foundation, for Christian proclamation. A denial of death is not
only a denial of the spirituals, but a denial of human history. But preaching to the needs of those dealing with death, pain, grief, and loss will have
"deep resonances" with the hearers because the sermon will touch their

human experience as it should.[138] Suffering is a part of the valley of the shadow of death, the valley of dry bones, thus preaching in a valley of dry bones requires that one remembers human tragedy while preaching. *Spiritual* preaching is not sorry for the sorrows of humanity because this is the way life is. As the spirituals did, pain is lamented, thus preaching laments the sorrows without forgetting the joys. The spirituals remind us that death must be dealt with in our preaching and not ignored. Our lives depend on it because, as Shawn Copeland says, "to pass over these sorrows imperils humanity as well as theology."[139] Even Christian theological memory includes a God who suffers.

Remembering God's Story

The second lesson from the spirituals that preachers can learn is that pain is even a part of God's story. To remember the spirituals reminds us of a God-in-the-flesh, Jesus Christ, who "never said a-mumblin word" as he suffered, bled, and died on a cross. The spirituals intone "Calvary, Calvary, Calvary, surely he died on Calvary." When one sings the spirituals, one has to deal with the reality of a God who dies because death is no respecter of persons. Even the Christ dies. "Were you there when they crucified my Lord? Were you there when they nailed him to the tree? Were you there when they pierced him in the side? Were you there when the sun refused to shine? Were you there when they laid him in the tomb?" The mantra of "Were you there?" brings you there, to the place of suffering and pain. It cannot be avoided even when one follows Jesus "lest our hearts, drunk with the wine of the world, we forget thee,"[140] including the memory of suffering and blood.

Our theological memory is washed in the blood of the Lamb. Preaching is not spoiled by tears for at the heart of the proclamation of the Christian church is a bloody death. As I noted earlier, eating the bread and drinking the cup of communion is a proclamation of the Lord's death. The eucharistic table is a table of death about a "lynched word," a "lynched black body."[141] Jesus died "gangsta-style," like all of the crucified peoples of the world. If the cross is our homiletical lens, then catastrophe and tragedy are at the heart of gospel preaching. He was terribly tortured, pierced in his side, nailed in his hands, and had a crown of thorns crushed on his head. He was bruised and broken, hung out to dry and die on an old rugged cross on a hill far away. With this theological lens, preaching has drops of blood all over it as preachers proclaim "a Lamb standing as if it had been slaughtered" (Rev. 5:6). The wounds of the crucifixion are not erased by the resurrection just as the wounds of centuries of brutality throughout the African diaspora are still present in psychological scars, mental slavery.

The presence of death is everywhere, even on the body of Christ, the lame Lamb. This perspective is not popular with the prosperity-gospel gurus nor with those who want to bleach the blood of Christ squeaky clean from hymnals. Through the spirituals, there is a convergence between slain ancestors and a slain Lamb that illuminates the weighty nature of preaching. This will be problematic to those who desire to praise without acknowledging pain. But the spirituals, musical sermons, affirm that pain is a part of preaching, humanly and divinely speaking. The intersection of cultural and theological memory is blood and death. Without the embrace of death in preaching, sermons are cheap. Preaching is costly because it is a matter of life and death. Death keeps Christianity real and connected to the way *spiritual* life really is. There are no resurrections without crucifixions.

This divine and human suffering, which is an aspect of God's story, is critical because it is the context of preaching. God enters the world and takes on its suffering, "not just regular suffering of all creatures that grow old and die, but the suffering of the innocent persecuted by the unjust, the suffering of abandonment and seeming failure, the suffering of love offered and refused, the suffering of evil apparently triumphant over good."[142] To avoid this kind of suffering is to ignore what it means to be human and what it means to serve an incarnate God. If memory is taken seriously for preaching, in the broken black bodies of the bards, one will discern the broken body of God on the cross, the heart of preaching. Christ's bones were crushed in his Golgotha valley of death and if the heart of preaching is the cross of Christ, the homiletical heart is a broken and bloody body. I can say, like Copeland, "These broken black bodies lie beside the body of the crucified Jesus on the altar of my heart."[143] Preachers should have an empathic heart toward death and suffering because of human and divine history; yet, this conversation about preaching and death does not mean that preachers need to bore people to death with their dried-up-like-a-raisin sermons or kill parishioners with judgmental ones. It does mean, however, that in preaching, we remember death and its reality honestly.

Remembering God's story via the spirituals also points us in more hopeful directions, as later chapters will emphasize. For now it suffices to note that the biblical literacy of the spirituals also suggests a God who delivers for the purpose of life. The spiritual "Didn't My Lord Deliver Daniel, Why Not Every Man?" remembers God's past action to empower individuals in the present. If God did it for Daniel, why not us? The spirituals were a way of affirming God's present action through affirmation of his past action. Through remembrance, one received a word of promise. In remembering Daniel, in this case, hope is discovered, intertwining memory and hope. Preaching that remembers the spirituals will find this hope in the past for the present, too. As the spiritual notes, "God is a God! God don't never change! God is a God an' he always will be God!" What God did in the past, God does in the present because God "don't never change." "He's jus de same today, Jus' de same today, an' de God dat lived in Daniel's time is jus de same today." This latter spiritual also replaces Daniel with Moses in one of the verses, which points to what has been called the "paradigmatic memory" for preaching—the exodus.[144]

Foremost (or at least close to the passion memory) in remembering the spirituals is the memory of the exodus. Indeed, this memory points to the pain of slavery and bondage in Egypt but it also gestures toward the liberatory actions of God who tells Moses to "go down" and tell Pharaoh, "Let my people go." Thus remembering the spirituals is not solely about death but also life, the life given to us by God. Yet, in our contemporary context, life is not on intravenous medicine because "life" is stressed at least in theory. It is death that is ignored and death is the starting place for preaching hope. Furthermore, appropriating the story of the exodus as their story allows African Americans to view themselves as God's people, the children of Israel. This memory provides a common history of death and hope. Africans Americans are a people who possess a collective identity even as revealed through the spirituals. The spirituals show that the experience of death (and life) is a communal embodied experience.

Remembering the Collective Body

The third lesson that the spirituals teach preachers is that tragedy, pain, struggle, and death are felt in the body of Christ, the *entire* community. *Spiritual* preaching includes everyone in the joys and sorrows. The fragrance in the valley of the "very many" dry bones is of an entire "slain" people (Ezek 37:9). Ezekiel paints the picture of a collective death and resurrection. If one suffers, all suffer. If one rejoices, all rejoice. A *people* endured much shame, sorrow, and death in the valley of oppression. Some suffer from cultural amnesia but an antidote to this amnesia is remembering the spirituals, the musical sermons that represent a miraculous response to the unjust setting of enslavement. Remembering slavery highlights that a group of people, individuals within a community, endured pain, which is why Allen Callahan can say, "Much of slave culture would be the keloids of collective consciousness."[145] A collective memory of the spirituals reminds preachers that all experience suffering on some level. The scars of the past remain in the present for a people as memories are passed down from one generation to the next. As humans we belong to "communities with histories,"[146] thus so-called individual experience is really a part of a larger communal narrative. The performance of call and response in the spirituals reveals the communal essence of African American communities, that when one suffers, all suffer. All engage in the pain because of what Paul Gilroy calls the "ethics of antiphony" that permeates the black Atlantic.[147]

Moreover, in this collective recollection, what is most important is the inclusive nature of community. These old songs carry a community's hope for freedom and justice. Preaching should occur out of the womb of a community's ideals. The community, the body of Christ, is the starting and ending point of a sermon so artfully depicted by Toni Morrison in her novel *Beloved*, when she writes, "Saying no more, [Baby Suggs] stood up then and danced with her twisted hip the rest of what her heart had to say while others opened their mouths and gave her the music."[148] Others provided the ending sermonic music for the preacher, Baby Suggs, who herself was a member of this ailing community. In this case, the wounded community finishes the sermon, preaches despite its pain, through its pain and agony. There is a rich intersubjective dynamic in a preaching community that goes beyond the performative dimensions.

As mentioned already, Johnson's "O Black and Unknown Bards" implies a communal creation of the spirituals with its unknown authors and origins. There are no specifics about the composer or lyricist because they are the community's sermons. Inherent in these songs is an opposition to an overly individualized contemporary culture that is more concerned with individual prosperity than community uplift and justice in society. The growth and health of a community is more significant than one's own maximization. The common good is more important than selfish individualism, which is why the unknown ones matter. The black bards created and led songs that were for the common good and not the glorification of the self. They themselves, according to Johnson, were "forgot." The fifth stanza of "O Black and Unknown Bards" reads:

>There is a wide, wide wonder in it all,
>That from degraded rest and service toil
>The fiery spirit of the seer should call
>These simple children of the sun and soil.
>O black slave singers, gone, forgot, unfamed,
>You—you alone, of all the long, long line
>Of those who've sung untaught, unknown, unnamed,
>Have stretched out upward, seeking the divine.

These singers, preachers without portfolio,[149] preach "far better than they knew" because their sermons sing on today for the life of a community. They did not preach for fame or fortune but for the survival of a people. Their lives call into question why preachers preach today. Is it for the fame of a television ministry and marketing privilege that grows one's followers and monetary offerings? Is it for the bigger car or larger house? Or, is it for ministry to those, like the black bards, who are "gone, forgot, unfamed . . . untaught, unknown, unnamed"? These whose names or faces are not known are the ones who have contributed to the history of the world, music, and preaching. They share homiletical pearls of wisdom. Those who are "unlettered," the underside, the marginalized, the other, teach preaching quite unlike any seminary or divinity school. Remembering the spirituals causes one to recognize a long line of unknown human beings as a valued part of the community. They, too, teach and preach and call us to listen to the *other*, those at the bottom rung of society. If they are excluded, authentic Christian preaching cannot happen because among the least of these is where Christ, the center of preaching, is found (Matthew 25). In this case, preaching lessons arise from these humble, "unfamed" domains of creativity. To forget them is to forget the roots of preaching and purpose of ministry. Preaching is a living memorial to those whose lives are "forgot" so easily.

The lives of the poor and unfamed, not just the lifestyles of the rich and famous, also should matter to preachers. The preaching bards call us to remember the suffering of those forgotten, unwanted, and unneeded, because they, too, are humans made in the image of God. God's community is wide and inclusive, challenging our sermons to do the same—to include those who are left out many times and bring the stories of the marginalized into the larger relational story of humanity and God. To talk about "dry bones" one has to engage those suffering most in society. The weak and powerless are foundational to an understanding of preaching that finds its power in a device of human torture, a cross. Those "gone" before have much to teach modern-day preachers who desire greatness because of a "drum major instinct."[150] The unknown and forgotten bards are great because they respect the least of these in the world and call preachers to minister to them, rather than blessing the corrupt empire of oppression that demonizes them. This preaching legacy of a community of have-nots leads one to resist the empires that dehumanize the poor, the jobless, and the homeless, the forgotten in society. Preaching in this communal tradition aims to help the listener re-member the human community by including all humans into this collective presence in the world. To forget the "forgot" is to forget what preaching is all about and who is at the heart of the gospel—an executed God who was on crucified lockdown.

The spirituals help preachers remember the most vulnerable among us so that no one would ever say, "I have no need of you" (1 Cor. 12:21), because each member of the human community is indispensable, even if they are unknown. One must go back to the place of death (e.g., slavery) in order to excavate life, to remember the past for the present and future, to make the unknown homiletically known to today's proclaimers of the gospel. The spirituals possess a wealth of homiletical wisdom that has not been tapped into as of yet, and the teachers' names are not even known. Moreover, they are "untaught" teachers without an enlightenment educational pedigree, but they are illumined by the Spirit, "the fiery spirit of the seer." Some so-called sophisticated preachers may want to ignore them because they were illiterate, ignorant, nonseminary-educated, premodern preaching bards; yet, Morrison sheds light on this when she talks about reading to her grandmother:

> And I have suspected, more often than not, that I *know* more than she did, that I *know* more than my grandfather and my great-grandmother did, but I also know that I'm no wiser than they were. And whenever I have tried earnestly to diminish their vision and prove to myself that I know more, and when I have tried to speculate on their interior life and match it up with my own, I have been overwhelmed every time by the richness of theirs compared to my own.[151]

The wisdom of the *spiritual* preachers is unmatched, though some may think otherwise. They expand notions of community and preaching and remind us of the humble roots of the gospel in the face of economically exploitative preaching practices. At their wellsprings of knowledge and at the altar of their souls, preachers may drink and bow to learn what one did not know or could not know about preaching without them. These voices preach from the past with melodies that should haunt our homiletical memory. They haunt homiletics because they call contemporary preachers to reclaim the weightiness of the call to preach.

Remembering the Weight of Preaching

The fourth lesson from the spirituals that preachers can learn is that the ministry of preaching is a matter of life and death. In other words, it is a weighty task. For the bards, they sang and preached to fight for life in the domain of death. Words were weapons of freedom and dignity. Just the "legacy of inhumanity"[152] that shapes these musical sermons should be enough to add weight to the task of preaching. To know that there was not "anything humorous"[153] about the nature or performance of the spirituals requires preachers to take preaching seriously. Preaching is not the latest joke to be told or funny story to be imagined or a hysterical shout to be heard. Remembering the spirituals reveals that there is much more at stake behind the sacred desk, the pulpit. Life and death are in the balance. Preaching as a form of resistance to deathly powers and a lifeline to an enslaved community reclaims the urgent impulse of proclamation. Because of the tremendous need of humanity, preaching requires a sense of urgency and passionate conviction that modern-day resurrections can arise from crucifixions, and there is healing for brokenness and strength for the weak. This kind of transformation will not come from the newest Facebook fad, fastest technological gadget, or the fanciest interactive church website, but from God. Life and wholeness from death and brokenness is God's specialty.

Dealing with a context of death requires God's presence and power. Preaching powered by the Holy Spirit is a miracle just like the spirituals, adding divine weight to this ministry of hope. Yet, many innovative preachers underestimate the power of God through words, thus they experiment with "fresh" ways of preaching that are powerless because they neglect to plug into the power of God. If preaching's purpose is to initiate life, bring justice, and affirm the dignity of all people, something more than a PowerPoint projection or a clever turn of phrase in a sermon is needed. The weight of preaching suggested by the spirituals indicates that God is needed and God is actually the one who provides preaching with the most weight. As Samuel Proctor says, "We deal with the deep center of human existence and the extreme outer perimeter. We are concerned with things that are ultimate."[154] God is ultimate and preachers who proclaim the gospel discern and name the eternal in our private and public affairs, life in the domain of little deaths. Even when facing the gallows of death, one could sing of the ever-present God, "Over my head, I hear music in the air. . . . There must be a God somewhere." The spirituals propel this notion of preaching and this should be affirmed because preachers "traverse terrain having to do with life and death."[155]

The spirituals challenge nonchalant, casual preaching in which nothing appears to be at stake, as if God will not be present in and through sermons. This kind of preaching does not recognize that life and death are in the power of the homiletical tongue. It ignores the *spiritual* foundation of preaching that demonstrates the weightiness of proclamation. Lightweight preaching is easily blown away by the slightest breeze of struggle into the sea of forgetfulness, leaving churches searching for other innovative ways to feed people. The real, weighty substance of the Bread of Life is absent. Lightweight sermons may tickle the ears of the congregation but will not reach the depths of their hearts nor usher Christ into their lives because there is no costly blood flowing through the preacher's homiletical veins, the blood of the cross. The spirituals want preachers to gain weight, the conviction that preaching is a matter of life and death in which everything is at stake.

Remembering the spirituals calls us to not repeat the past of human oppression but to preach in solidarity with the oppressed. Weighty preaching requires that the preacher put everything on the line for others, even his or her own body and life. Preaching necessitates a holistic approach not only to resist the powers of death but to help others discern "eternity bending low all around us."[156] The weight of preaching resides at the intersection of eternity and humanity, divinely authorized for some human good. The spirituals help us to reclaim this view of preaching the gospel. But to gain weight in our preaching, one must not be afraid or hesitant to remember the past, for there is much to be learned from it, as the spirituals reveal.

As noted earlier, there are various reasons why people do not want to remember the past. Some take the view of Paul D, in *Beloved,* who tells Sethe, "Me and you, we got more yesterday than anybody, we need some kind of tomorrow."[157] The past has been too painful and one does not want to relive or remain in the past through memory because memory keeps the past alive. Others like Fred Shuttlesworth, Baptist minister and former leader of Southern Christian Leadership Conference, believe, "If you don't tell it like it was, it can never be as it ought to be."[158] For him, truthful recounting of the past is the pathway toward a better future. There is an obvious tension about remembering the past of death and suffering and this should not be taken lightly. But, "remembering is the preacher's *duty*."[159] In fact, "the entire substance of Christianity, since Christ has not reappeared on earth, consists in the remembrance of his life and teachings."[160] If a preacher celebrates forgetting the past, this is something to be lamented because in that forgetting, the gospel story itself will be forgotten. Fred Craddock names remembering as essential for the ministry of preaching when he says, "If you're too young to remember, then you're not old enough to preach."[161] Craddock is talking about the spiritual maturity of a preacher. Embracing memory as critical to the practice represents how well one is prepared or not to preach.

Memory not only shapes the identity of a community but also of preachers.[162] It affects not only what one does in sermons but who one is in living the sermon. A forgetful preacher might likely neglect the valley of dry bones that has wedged its path throughout past and present human history. The exodus and the passion of Christ may have no impact on this kind of preacher because they have forgotten the significance of those events and do not realize their critical presence even in the spirituals. Human tragedy and death, God's story of death, the forgotten ones in the human community, and the weighty nature of preaching, may be overlooked for lighter and brighter sermonic possibilities; but, to re-member the future of the church and preaching, one must remember the past depicted by the spirituals. "Memory is not only a source of information about the past but also a force in creating the future."[163] As a force, "it breaks into the present and gains a new lease on life."[164] Remembering (death) provides life in the present and for the future. This is a "hermeneutics of memory"[165] that actually leads to what I will call the "hermeneutics of hope" in chapter 4. To remember the dismembered is to re-member the future of preaching in the valley of dry bones. Memory funds Christian preaching.

A preacher remembers "the days when hope unborn had died" in order to prevent another miscarriage of hope. Preaching midwifes hope into the world, and when it is born it will not disappoint (Rom. 5:5). However, "Hope depends upon living memory made palpable."[166] This link between hope and the memory of death, specifically, will become more obvious in the next chapter through a discussion of the relationship between death and hope in the spirituals.

2

Hear the Word of the Lord

The Content of *Spirit*ual Preaching

> O dry bones, hear the word of the LORD.
>
> —EZEK. 37:4

> I'm gonna preach when the Spirit says a-preach
>
> —TRADITIONAL

Remembering the spirituals not only aids the perspective that death is the context of preaching, but also reveals the significance of the Spirit in preaching. The spirituals suggest an intermingling of the Spirit, death, and hope. This is important especially for those who desire to preach in the Spirit. Through the lens of the spirituals, if preaching is a "living, breathing, flesh and blood expression of a theology of the Holy Spirit,"[1] two vital components of the content of Spirit-filled proclamation, or what I call *spiritual preaching*, are death and hope. This chapter will explore the Spirit, death, and hope as found in the spirituals as a way of reflecting on what it really means to preach in the Spirit. Death may be the context of preaching in the valley of dry bones, but the Spirit provides the power and substance of that preaching, embracing death while animating hope.

Ezekiel and the Spirit

Ezekiel in the valley of dry bones as a homiletical metaphor suggests the importance of the Spirit in the preaching ministry. Just as prominent as the images of death in Ezekiel 37 is the source of life, specifically the Hebrew word for "spirit," "breath," or "wind": *ruach*. It occurs ten times in this passage and it is the main theological motif in this context of death. Death and Spirit play significant roles where Ezekiel is called to prophesy, to preach, in the same way that the presence of death and the Spirit exist in our congregations. Facing death courageously reveals a deep trust in the Spirit, for as Ezekiel says, "[God] brought me out by the spirit of the LORD and set me down in the middle of a valley" of dry bones (v. 1), in the middle of death and contamination. The Spirit brings him to the place of death and contamination to preach, to take a risk for the life of a community; if one is not ready to face death, one is not ready to preach because preaching is a matter of life and death. It is critical to note, especially for those who only see the Spirit in the mountaintops of life and moments of prosperity, that the Spirit is also present in the lowest of valleys, even the valleys of dry bones. The Spirit is there in the homiletical domain of death and is the one who nudges us to proclaim a word of the Lord in the midst of death. In other words, the Spirit of life resides in the valley of the shadow of death. Thus one might say that an embrace of death is an embrace and invocation of the Spirit, because by risking contamination and death by engaging it, preachers demonstrate their hope for resurrection and new life. Preachers must risk death to bestow life.

When Ezekiel prophesies to the dead, dry bones, it is clear that the "breath" or "spirit" is linked to new life, because wherever he mentions these terms, except in verse 1, he follows it by saying "you shall live" (vv. 5, 6, 14), or "they may live" (v. 9), or "they lived" (v. 10). The Spirit of God is the source of new life and hope, not any human being or preacher. One's preaching does not bring salvation but the Spirit working through one's preaching initiates it. Even when the "bones came together, bone to its bone" (v. 7) with sinews, flesh, and skin, there was no life, no breath, no spirit initially (v. 8), though we hear what one scholar calls, "a grand rattle of recreation."[2] There are just empty shells of flesh, zombies, until the breath or spirit of life is imparted to these once dead people (vv. 9-10), painting a reenactment of the primal act of creation, when God formed humanity from the dust of the ground and breathed into their nostrils the breath of life (Gen. 2:7). As in Genesis, it is true here—God is the source of life and revivification. The many dry bones were "lying in the valley" (v. 2), but because of the inspiration of the spirit of God, the "vast multitude" eventually "stood on their feet" (v. 10). They were down but through the Spirit, they got up.

This is nothing less than a scene of resurrection by the power of the breath, spirit, of God. That it is a resurrection is confirmed with the images of graves (vv. 12-13), which will be further discussed in chapter 4. For now, it suffices to say that only God's Spirit can bring life out of death (Deut. 32:39) and in this vision, it happens in conjunction with prophesying or preaching. Christian preaching is not only life-giving but hope-restoring. In this case, the "vast multitude" is "the whole house of Israel" who had lamented, "Our hope is lost" (v. 11). Ezekiel reveals that through the Spirit, hope is restored out of death. To land at a place of hope, one has to go *through* a place of death. In both death and hope, the Spirit is present because "it is not possible to explore the spirit of life without facing squarely the reality of death."[3] The Spirit leads preachers to a context of death to animate hope and life. This becomes even clearer through the close connection between the Spirit and the *spirit*uals.

The Spirit and the *Spirit*uals

Stemming from the Spirit

Ezekiel was not the only one who knew about the Spirit in death. The spirituals demonstrate the presence of the Spirit in a domain of death. These musical sermons were fused with the presence of the Spirit. The religion of the slave consisted of "the Preacher, the Music, and the Frenzy"[4] or, in other words, preaching, music, and the Spirit. All three of these categories converge in the spirituals because they are musical sermons inspired by the Spirit. This should not be surprising because "African American religion based on spirituals emphasizes the role of the Holy Ghost."[5] From the very beginning with the creation of the "spirituals," the Spirit was deemed to be present. Indeed, the "spirituals" are called such because they stem from the Spirit. They are musical sermonic revelations of the Spirit. Bernice Johnson Reagon affirms this belief when she declares that these religious songs are called spirituals "because they came from the spirit—deep within."[6] All music, including folk songs, in African traditions could be viewed as "spiritual" because there is not a divide between the sacred and secular realms, but "spirituals" usually refer to songs that have an obvious religious theme, drawing on the Bible. Differentiating between possible genres of folk songs is not pertinent to this project but what is important is that slave songs, particularly the musical sermons called "spirituals," were believed to have a divine origin. Thus we have the name *spirit*ual.

God the Spirit gave blacks these musical sermons called the spirituals; thus they may be called *spiritual preaching*, that is, Spirit-filled proclamation. The Spirit enabled slaves to preach under crushing circumstances. Without God, there would be no sermon. Without God, there would be no song.[7] The divine Spirit sparks these singing sermons. "When the spirit moved, one of their singers would uplift a mighty voice, like a bard of old . . ."[8] The Spirit is linked to singing even in the Bible, affirming the relationship between the spirituals and the Spirit (cf. Eph. 5:18-20). This relationship causes William Turner to declare, "The pervasive undertone supplied by music is correlative to the presence and movement of the Spirit which empowers every authentic word of preaching." For him, the music of black preaching is "singing in the spirit."[9] The music of preaching is a sign of the Spirit because the Spirit sings through spiritual preachers, then and now. What these songs preach stems from a spiritual source and in the Spirit, singing is preaching and preaching is singing.

If the spirituals are musical sermons of the Spirit, spiritual preaching, then what they proclaim comes from the Spirit. Studying the spirituals will help modern-day preachers learn what it means to preach in the Spirit. The unknown black bards' lips touched the sacred fire. James Weldon Johnson writes,

> There is a wide, wide wonder in it all,
> That from degraded rest and service toil
> The fiery spirit of the seer should call
> These simple children of the sun and soil.[10]

Johnson connects the fire, spirit, and seer to the call of the bards to create spirituals much in the same way that the Spirit is linked to prophecy throughout the Bible. The fiery lyrics of the bards are words of the Spirit, inspirited texts and sounds. The bards are prophets in their own right, touched by the fire of the Spirit to preach the gospel truth.

This does not mean that every musical sermon, every spiritual, has to say "spirit," because just to say "spirit" does not mean one preaches in the Spirit nor is it an indication of one's own relationship with the Spirit. In fact, there are few direct references to the Spirit in the spirituals.[11] The spirituals, like preaching, imply pneumatology. It is more appropriate to think about the spirituals as the expressive voice of the Spirit preaching through humanity with particular words and sounds because "the spirituals usually assume the pervasive presence of the Holy Spirit with the believer . . ."[12] The Spirit permeates the entirety of the spiritual, even without being explicitly named; thus the content of *spirit*ual preaching requires lyrical and acoustical sensitivity. The sound of preaching matters, not just the words. How something is said is as important as what is said. This is especially true in black expressions of music and preaching.

Sounding the Spirit

The story of High John De Conqueror who came on the "waves of sound" and noted that God gave the slaves a "tune" without words should suggest the importance of sound in black religion, including preaching about death and hope. Black religion is "a sounding religion."[13]

The sounds of the spirituals say something about the Spirit who gave the sound. There is no sound without breath, *ruach*, spirit. The *spirit*uals are Spirit speech. The biblical witness points to an integral connection between the Spirit and sound, therefore, the significance of sound in African American preaching traditions implies a welcome of the presence of the Spirit in this manner.[14] African Americans "move with sounds."[15]

The tunes of the spirituals themselves preached a message. Reagon says, "In a system like slavery, where open critique is dangerous, the spirituals by their sound become a dissenting voice."[16] A word came through spiritual sounds. Frederick Douglass experienced the spirituals in this way:

> They told a tale of woe, which was then altogether beyond my feeble comprehension; they were tones, loud, long, and deep; breathing the prayer and complaint of souls boiling over with the bitterest anguish. Every tone was a testimony against slavery, and a prayer to God for deliverance from chains. The hearing of those wild notes always depressed my spirit, and filled me with ineffable sadness. I have frequently found myself in tears while hearing them.[17]

The tones of these musical sermons lead to Douglass's tears because the sounds are full of meaning. They are not empty echoes of nothingness. When one hears or sings sounds, one feels in the body; acoustemology involves physiology, especially in black religion when one might say, "Don't give me no religion I can't feel."[18] Singing and preaching run sound through the body of the speaker and listener. Thus a study of the spirituals for the purpose of preaching involves attention to sound but it also entails awareness of the physical nature of sounding the Spirit. In his study of the spirituals, *Wade in the Water*, Arthur Jones affirms this when he writes that it is "impossible to gain a full understanding of the spirituals from an examination of song lyrics alone, without hearing (and especially singing) the rhythms and melodies of the songs as well."[19] One does not fully understand the preaching of the gospel without taking into consideration how it sounds. This is particularly true for African American churches because for many blacks, as was the case with Paul Robeson, they may say, "I hear my way through the world."[20] If the importance of the Spirit and sound in the musical preaching of the spirituals is that significant for understanding them better, then for my purpose of thinking about preaching death and hope, one should ask, "What do we listen for in the spirituals?"

Paying attention to the sound of the spirituals is attentiveness to the contour of the Spirit in preaching death and hope. As Robert Beckford writes, "Sound is not merely noise; it is fecund with cultural values."[21] Jeremy Begbie, Don Saliers, and others would say sound is also fecund with theological meaning.[22] Stephen Webb asserts that there is "a soundscape to Christian theology."[23] The spirituals demonstrate that there is a soundscape to homiletical theology, including death and hope; a hasty listener may not be attuned to this. How death and hope sound speaks volumes about what they mean in the preaching moment. The soundscape of the spirituals may shed light on the concepts of death and hope. The texts will be studied, but so will the subtexts when helpful to this conversation. The triadic relationship of the sonic, somatic, and pneumatic requires such subtextual investigation.

I must admit that it is difficult to capture on the page that which occurs off the page in sound and gesture. Nonetheless, in the following discussion about how the spirituals preach about death and hope, I will include insights about the acoustical dynamics of certain spirituals alongside the lyrical dynamics where that will further understanding. Thus the content of *spirit*ual preaching is both textual and tonal. In terms of acoustics, the discussion will include the following performative dimensions of the spirituals: rhythm, repetition, antiphony, and melody. These characteristics, along with the actual lyrics, will shed light on how the Spirit(ual) preaches death and hope and will aid preachers in listening to and learning from this spiritual homiletical tradition.

Musical Homiletical Theology of the Spirit(uals)

Communal Embodiment

In thinking about the theo-musical, theo-rhetorical make-up of spiritual preaching, it is critical to remember the deep sense of and yearning for community within these musical sermons. There is always "room for many a mo'." These sermons represent a transparent example of the Spirit inhabiting a people, a temple (1 Corinthians 3), through the sounds and words of a song. Like the imagery of Ezekiel, the Spirit instigates a collective revival. Death and hope are experienced by the community. Thus the spirituals represent first and foremost an embodied, communal theology of the Spirit. This is not necessarily explicit but implicit through antiphonal performance and the unknown origins of these songs. Spiritual preaching is an "intragroup thing"[24] and representative of "an African American communal voice."[25] In interpreting death and hope in the spirituals, the community takes priority; thus death and hope are ultimately communal. What happens to one is experienced by all. The musical homiletical theology is for the life of a community, including today's preachers.

Thus the following excursus will focus on the interrelation of death and hope in the spirituals as a way of exploring what this might mean for contemporary preaching. This is not to say that the spirituals do not ever speak of death or hope singularly without any interaction with the other because this is not the case. But due to the limited scope of this book, I will center on those musical sermons that voice both death and hope in the same sermonic song. That interaction will help us in this study of what it means to preach death *and* hope and why this is significant.

Death and Hope in Spiritual Preaching

Before taking a closer look at the actual text and music of some spirituals, some preliminary remarks are in order. It should be clear that the enslaved lived the blues in a "valley of heartache."[26] However, they were not alone because the divine presence of the Spirit was with them, singing and preaching through them via the spirituals in the valley of death. In fact, George Cummings writes,

> the lives of black slaves, according to their testimonies, were filled with the consequences of the presence of the Spirit: secret meetings, which are an expression of independence; disobeying their masters in order to serve God in prayer and worship; getting practical tools to help with confronting life; hope; visions of freedom; and physical manifestations of being possessed by the Spirit. In the midst of the dialectic of struggle and hope black slaves attributed their hope to the Spirit of God.[27]

Any signs of hope were from the Spirit though this hope did not erase their situation of death. "Death was a fact of existence which could become a reality at the slightest whim of slave masters; but since God is the sovereign ruler, death cannot be the master of life."[28] Death and life are aspects of the truth that must be told in preaching, but God's presence makes all the difference, which the spirituals reveal. In *The Negro Spiritual Speaks of Life and Death*, Howard Thurman says, "Death was a fact, inescapable, persistent. For the slave, it was extremely compelling because of the cheapness with which his life was regarded. . . . He was faced constantly with the imminent threat of death, of which the terrible overseer was the symbol; . . . If a slave were killed, it was merely a property loss, a matter of bookkeeping."[29] Despite this fact, Thurman tells us of another conviction and "fact of life" that trumped the reality of death. He says,

> What, then, is the fundamental significance of all these interpretations of life and death? What are these songs trying to say? They express the profound conviction that God was not done with them, that God was not done with life. The consciousness that God had not exhausted His resources or better still that the vicissitudes of life could not exhaust God's resources, did not ever leave them. This is the secret of their ascendency over circumstances and the basis of their assurances concerning life and death. The awareness of the presence of a God who was personal, intimate and active was the central fact of life and around it all the details of life and destiny were integrated.[30]

Death is a fact in spiritual preaching but so is God. The inevitability of death shines through the spirituals though it is not welcomed per se. Death is a "robber" in one case. "Death ain't nothin' but a robber, don't you see. . . . Death came to my house, he didn't stay long, I looked in the bed an' my mother was gone, Death ain't nothin' but a robber, don't you see." Death "comes a-creapin" and even comes to Jesus, as revealed in the numerous spirituals about his death. Yet, Wyatt Tee Walker reminds us that despite the vicissitudes of life "hope was always the Spiritual's central theme."[31] The irony is that the term *hope* is rarely, if ever, used in a spiritual, revealing that hope is not generated by articulating the word. Hope in spiritual preaching bubbles up when death is not fixated upon and viewed as the whole gospel story; rather, death is viewed in the light of the presence of an active God who makes ways out of no ways. Hope comes when one believes that there is more than death to life. Even if a spiritual does not preach an obvious word of hope, it is important to remember that the sermonic song itself is a sign of hope because "hope is a song in a weary throat."[32]

Death as Necessary Climate for Hope. In exploring death and hope in the spiritual homiletical tradition, one of the places to begin is with the observation that the experience of death or little deaths is the starting point for the hopeful desire for something better. Death is the necessary climate for the expression of hope. One might argue that hope would not be voiced or desired if the individual or community was not experiencing some type of pain. A song may be hope but it is *only* hope with the vital presence of a "weary throat," demonstrating a connection to human struggle and pain. In one spiritual, "My Body Rock 'Long Fever," the speaker declares: "O my body rock 'long fever, O! wid a pain in 'e head! / I wish I been to de kingdom, to sit along side o' my Lord!"

The pain in the head and the fever create a space for the desire to be in the kingdom with the Lord. The singing preacher wishes to be in another world because of the hardship in this present world. The fever and pain establish a climate out of which hope for something else arises. In this musical sermon, the melody hits the highest note (E), the climax, on the word *pain*. In fact, "O! wid a pain in 'e head" has the highest notes in the entire song. Pain gets the most attention as hope for the kingdom gradually declines musically. The little deaths, pain, are the most excruciating and seemingly rise triumphant even over the hope in this situation. This is true to the way life often is when death appears to be dominant and hope is muted. The music of this spiritual embodies this. Nonetheless, hope is voiced, though not as strongly as death.

In "Lis'en to De Lam's," lyrical repetition in the refrain is used to accentuate the reality of death.

> Lis'en to de lam's, all a-cryin'
> Lis'en to de lam's, all a-cryin'
> Lis'en to de lam's, all a-cryin'
> I wan'ta go to heaben wen I die.

Lambs, humanity, cry out. This point cannot be missed. The singing preacher gets more specific in the verses. He or she says,

> Come on sister wid yo' ups an' downs,
>> wan'ta go to heaben wen I die.
> De angel's waitin' for to give you a crown,
>> wan'ta go to heaben wen I die.
> Come on mourner an'a don't be shame,
>> wan'ta go to heaben wen I die.
> De angel's waitin' for to write-a yo' name,
>> wan'ta go to heaben wen I die.
> Mind out brother how you walk de cross,
>> wan'ta go to heaben wen I die.
> Yo' foot might slip-a an' yo' soul get-a los',
>> wan'ta go to heaben wen I die.

There are ups and downs and mourning with the ongoing pulse to "wan'ta go to heaben when I die." The redundancy of crying humanity is met with this repetitive desire to go to heaven upon one's death. One wants heaven but death is the first act that must occur, according to this spiritual. All of the crying and struggles, the little deaths, are a precursor to going to heaven, but those circumstances create a climate in which the "longing toward a truer world"[33] happens. That longing comes from dissatisfaction with the current state of affairs. Death is clearly inevitable—"*wen* I die." The recognition of our ultimate death, even the little deaths that lead to the final death, are necessary for the expression of hope ("wan'ta go to heaben") to happen.

Death as a transitional place and context leading toward hope is poignantly demonstrated in such imagery as "the River Jordan" in the spirituals. Albert Raboteau notes that "most frequently Death was, in the spirituals, the River Jordan, the last river to cross before reaching Canaan, the promised home for which the weary travelers had toiled so long."[34] Many spirituals speak of crossing the Jordan to the promised land, suggesting that one has to cross death's domain to get to the other side, the land of hope. Thus, "Roll Jordan Roll" is a call to go through death to roll over into hope. Death is the climate, the milieu, out of which hope comes.

Death as the Hope. But death is not just the climate essential for hope to happen. At times, spiritual preaching views death as the hope. Because of the extreme suffering endured by the enslaved, death, even the final death, was deemed better than the life they lived on earth. One can sense the relief experienced through death in this spiritual: "Now we take this feeble body, And we carry it to the tomb, And we all leave it there—Hallelujah." God is praised (Hallelujah) for the rest one finds in the darkness of death's tomb. Another spiritual, through its lyrical repetition and melodic landscape, reveals a similar sentiment. "Death, oh death, oh me Lawd, Death, oh death, oh me Lawd. When-a me body lay down in de grave, Den-a me soul gwine shout fo' joy." Not only is the notion of death emphasized through the obvious repetition of "death" but the melodic notes soar on "death" above any mention of joy. Both of these characteristics accentuate the yearning for death as release from a world of toil and sorrow. An ultimate death was better than the life of a slave, a status that itself was a little death. At least, one could maintain a sense of human dignity through death. Through the finality of death, one hoped for freedom from the bondage of slavery, an earthly death. This desire for death was a form of resistance to the death experienced in slavery. "Oh, freedom! Oh, freedom! Oh, freedom all over me! An' be fo' I'd be a slave, I'll be buried in my grave, an' go home to ma Lawd an' be free." The grave, a sign of death, was the portal to freedom for many. Death was viewed as the only hope in these cases.[35]

Even certain images in the spirituals such as the "train" represent both death and life or hope, implicitly making death the hope. The spiritual "Same Train" says,

> Same train, same train, same train, carry my mother,
> Same train, same train, same train, carry my mother;
> Same train, be back tomorrer, same train, same train.

The repetition of the words "same train" in conjunction with the repeated rhythm each time suggests the inevitability of the coming of death. It will "be back tomorrer" suggests that it is a daily occurrence. However, the train figure is not just an image of death but also one of hope as in the spiritual "Git on board, little chillen, Git on board, little chillen, Git on board, little chillen, Dere's room for many a mo! De gospel train's a-comin', I hear it jus' at han; I hear de car wheels movin', An' rumblin' thro de lan', Git on board, little chillen . . . " That train is death but it is also hope and good news thus the singing preacher invites others to "git on board." The train metaphor is another example of death as the hope.

Hope in and despite Death. Death as the hope is not the most popular approach to the relationship of death and hope in spiritual preaching. The more prominent paradigm is the expression of hope in and despite the experience of death. This is where one might discern the dogged faith embedded in these cultural musical sermons. James Earl Massey teaches that the "deep substructure of the spirituals . . . is faith," a "faith in the creative, all-powerful, delivering, sustaining, energizing, and fulfilling activity of a just and loving God."[36] Faith in God is critical for generating hope in the spirituals. Without the presence of God in the midst of the presence of death, there would not be the voice of faith and hope. Hope in death arises because God is at work on earth and has a proven track record throughout history. "God is a God! God don't never change! God is a God an' he always will be God!" This spiritual stresses "God" through repetition and this is the ultimate reason for the hope in harsh times. God is omnipresent and omnipotent. There is a firm belief that what God did in the past, God does in the present because "God don't never change." The same God who saved Moses and Daniel is the same God at work today. One spiritual asserts this explicitly in its repetitive refrain: "Is jus de same today, Jus' de same today, an' de God dat lived in Moses' [or Daniel's] time is jus de same today." Despite the apparent odds, the core theological belief of the enslaved was "that God had not left them alone, and that God would set them free from human bondage."[37]

God is the deliverer, the one who initiates liberation and freedom in the confines of death, revealing that hope is ultimately in God. In the antiphonal "Go Down, Moses," it is God who instructs Moses to go and "Tell ole Pharaoh, Let my people go." The cry of freedom, "Let my people go," is emphasized not only through repetition of melody and rhythm but through the community singing this portion of the song in response to the leader. Through the community's involvement at this moment, this sermonic song aims to grab our attention at this point of liberation, even in the higher volume that would be natural as these words are sung by a group. What we have in this musical sermon is the notion that "liberation [is] consistent with divine revelation."[38] In the midst of Egyptian oppression, God comes to stir hope: "Let my people go." Another spiritual that has the exodus motif is "Wade in the Water," which uses antiphonal verses as the community responds on "God's a-gonna trouble the water." That is the main idea of communal hope in these troubling waters of the Red Sea—God will intervene in the domain of struggle and death. God will trouble our trouble, giving new meaning to "double trouble." The weight of hope rests in the presence of God. Despite cruel circumstances, spiritual preaching proclaims "There must be a God somewhere." In other words, "there is at the heart of life a Heart."[39]

Faith in God was vital for hope to be experienced in death but one must be careful not to romanticize slave Christianity and the spirituals because not all slaves believed in God or were "Christian."[40] Yet, the spirituals provide overwhelming evidence of a belief in a divine presence such that hope can arise in the midst of pain and agony.

The expression of hope comes not only in situations of death, but despite death being so pervasive.

> Nobody knows the trouble I see,
> Nobody knows my sorrow;
> Nobody knows the trouble I see,
> Glory, hallelujah!

In this classic spiritual, the little deaths are noted the most, three times, in this refrain. That one is in trouble is made clear through lyrical and melodic repetition. However, *despite* the fact that "nobody knows," this singer seems to suggest that there is Someone who does and concludes with a note of triumph and praise: "Glory, hallelujah!" In fact, the melody rises on "glory" suggesting that hope triumphs ultimately, rising above the pain and trouble. That particular note is the highest in the refrain. The music leads the singer to that climax of hopeful sound, prefiguring the final resolution of God for the world. Just as this spiritual has direction, eschatology is about the future direction of the Christian faith in which there is fulfillment of God's purposes for the creation.[41] This musical sermon demonstrates that in the end, despite the ongoing death, hope will win and declare "Glory, hallelujah."

The movement toward hope in this spiritual affirms what Du Bois notices about these musical sermons: "Through all of the sorrow of the Sorrow Songs there breathes a hope—a faith in the ultimate justice of things. The minor cadences of despair change often to triumph and calm confidence."[42] The triumphant "Glory, hallelujah!" stands out in what might be considered a sad refrain. Hope rises despite the sadness. "Soon-a Will Be Done" moves in a similar way with its words and music. The pulsating rhythm and repetition in conjunction with the prominent "troubles of the world" in the refrain depicts the ongoing nature of trouble and the bumpiness of life. It would appear that trouble has triumphed over any hope but just as in "Nobody Knows the Trouble I See," the singing preacher concludes in the refrain with "Goin' home to live with God," which happens to be the highest notes in the refrain, giving hope the last word again. The little deaths in life are not eternal. At some point in God's purposes, there will be "no more weeping and a-wailing." Spiritual preaching basically proclaims "it is my 'termination for to hold out to the end" because in the end, hope prevails. As Thurman asserts, "the great idea about death itself is that it is not *the master of life*. It may be inevitable, yes; gruesome, perhaps; releasing, yes; but triumphant, never. With such an affirmation ringing in their ears, it became possible for them, slaves though they were, to stand anything that life could bring against them."[43] The power of hope permeates spiritual preaching yet one is still realistic about the "sad joyfulness"[44] of human reality.

Many of the spirituals reveal the mixed texture of life. One verse of "Nobody Knows the Trouble I See" says truthfully, "Sometimes I'm up, sometimes I'm down . . ." The ups and downs of life, the already-not yet eschatological tension of the Christian life, are present. This creative dialogical tension is made explicit in the following spiritual:

> Chilly water, chilly water, Hallelujah to dat Lam'.
> I know that water is chilly and cold, An' a Hallelujah to dat Lam'.
> But I have Jesus in my soul, An' a Hallelujah to dat Lam'.
> Satan's jes' like a snake in de grass. An' a Hallelujah to dat Lam'.
> He's watching for to bite you as-a you pass, An' a Hallelujah
> to dat Lam'.

Despite the somber "chilly water," the cold river of death, or other obstacles in life such as Satan, "hallelujah" is voiced. The melody on the repetition of "Hallelujah to dat Lam'" is repeated and remains sure, bouncing with confidence every time in the face of hard times. There is an ebb and flow between little deaths and the expression of praise and hope. They are interwoven in this song just as in life. Death is not erased but present even as one preaches the hope of "hallelujah." The joyful sorrow of the spirituals is obvious in other spirituals as well. In the famous "Balm in Gilead," the verses exude this relationship. For now, verse one suffices as exemplary of the movement and structure of each lyrical verse: "Sometimes I feel discouraged, and think my work's in vain, / But then the Holy Spirit revives my soul again." Each verse is a reminder of the reality of death in its varied forms but concludes with the reality of hope. The refrain gives hope priority in the end by stating, "There is a balm in Gilead, to make the wounded whole / There is a balm in Gilead, to heal the sin-sick soul." The powers of death may be strong but the singing preacher proclaims "There is a balm in Gilead" in the face of death. These musical sermons are a true representation of life—true to human suffering and the reality of God. As mentioned already, there is hope that "trouble don't last always" because of the presence of God. The "hallelujahs" that resound are praises to God, implying the presence of God in the midst of suffering and death. These sermons may be "born of tears and suffering greater than any formula of expression. And yet the authentic note of triumph in God rings out trumpet-tongued!"[45] This "God sense" is what leads William McClain to sum up African American singing in this manner:

> In our melancholy, our songs are not always mournful songs. Most often, they are joyous, lifting the spirit above despair. Yet, our sad songs sometimes come in the midst of our joy, in moments of jubilation and celebration. Without warning caution emerges to remind us that songs of joy must be tempered by the stark realities of the plight of our people. In the midst of our joyful singing the soul has not forgotten depression, pain, and expressions of hopelessness on the faces of our young. Laughter turns to tears and our glad songs into laments. But we refuse to give up or give in. There is a God sense that has become a part of the fabric of the race. We refuse to let God alone, and we know God has never let us alone! At the moment of our deepest despair we sing, 'sometimes I feel like a motherless child a long way from home.' Then, in the midst of our sadness, we sing with assurance, 'I'm so glad that trouble don't last always!'[46]

In death, despite death, hope sings with dogged determination. "I've been 'buked an' I've been scorned, Dere is trouble all over dis worl', Ain' gwine lay my 'ligion down." Furthermore, hope sings of a journey to a heavenly home.

Hope (and Death) on a Journey to a Heavenly Home. It is important to recognize that death and hope are experiences on the journey of life. The spirituals preach a message that this world is not our home but that we are pilgrims passing through this land. Thurman writes that for the enslaved, "Life is regarded as a pilgrimage, a sojourn, while the true home of the spirit is beyond the vicissitudes of life with God."[47] On a journey or pilgrimage, blacks sing, even as accompaniment to loved ones' sojourn home to God. Singing "covers [blacks] from cradle to coffin."[48] The idea of a progressing journey, eventually arriving at one's destination, stands out in the spirituals. Death and hope are parts of the process as one travels so we hear, "Let us cheer the weary traveler, cheer the weary traveler, Let us cheer the weary traveler, along the heavenly way. . . . An' brothers, if you meet with crosses, an' trials on the way, just keep your trust in Jesus, an' don't forget to pray." One needs encouragement, to be cheered on, in a wearisome world. There will be crosses to bear on the pilgrimage but there is movement "toward a divine fulfillment."[49] Hope does not deny historical realities but accepts them. That one is moving at all is a sign of hope. "Keep a-inchin' along, Keep a-inchin' along, Massa Jesus is comin' bye an' bye, Keep a-inchin' along like po' inch worm, Massa Jesus is comin' bye and bye." One inches along, believing that Jesus is coming. One keeps moving as hope propels one forward.

The sense of movement toward a goal shines through many of the spirituals, particularly in those that use the image of water and sailing ships or boats—"Michael row de boat a-shore, Hallelujah!" "Sail, O believer, sail, Sail over yonder," "One mo' river to cross." The rowing, sailing, and crossing, signify a journey. The journey is not stagnant but moves in a specific trajectory. Other musical sermons use different imagery to depict the journey of life. But regardless of the imagery, the singers' basic message is "I will go, I shall go, to see what the end will be." When the "going" is gone, there is no possibility of hope, but only death. The going, the movement itself, signifies hope even in an "unfriendly world" of little deaths.

The journey, as noted, has a particular direction. For the unknown black bards, they were "goin' home to live with God." Home was viewed as the final destination for the slave singing preachers. Many spirituals speak of "home," which should not be surprising coming from those who had been separated from their loved ones and homeland. They yearned for home even though they felt like motherless children "a long ways from home." Despite the distance from home, they were determined to return there because home was a place for community. At home, they would not be lonely but see mother, father, sister, brother, and, of course, God. Home was the context to reestablish relationships that had been severed and a place of freedom finally—to "go home to ma Lawd and be free." Some call "Swing Low, Sweet Chariot" a "cradle-song of death,"[50] but it can also be viewed as a song of hope as one prepares to travel home: "Swing low, sweet chariot, Coming for to carry me home." One anticipates going home and does not resist it as the community embraces going home in their response to the call of the leader on each verse and in the refrain with the same rhythmic words—"coming for to carry me home." Home sounds like good news as one deals with life; thus a black bard could sing, "Until I reach-a ma home, Until I reach-a ma home, I nevah inten' to give de journey ovah, until I reach-a ma home." The ongoing journey of hope toward home was worth it because at home, the final resting place,

> Dere's no rain to wet you. O yes, I want to go home, want to go home. . . . Dere's no sun to burn you. . . . Dere's no hard trials . . . no whips a-crackin'. . . no stormy weather . . . no tribulation . . . no more slavery in de kingdom . . . no evil-doers in de kingdom . . . all is gladness in de kingdom. . . . O yes, I want to go home, want to go home.

At home, there was an absence of trouble and death and only gladness. In other words, home was heaven.

The notion of heaven is muted in much of today's preaching[51] but in the spirituals, heaven was prominent. "I'm gwine to my heaven, I'm gwine home; Archangel open de door." Spirituals like "Poor Rosy" said repeatedly, "Heav'n shall-a be my home." Heaven was not yet reached but was longed for on the journey. This longing for a heavenly home did not ignore the facts of the real world, the little deaths. "There is no attempt to cast a false glow over the stark ruggedness of the journey."[52] "City Called Heaven" is a case in point:

> I am a poor pilgrim of sorrow,
> I'm tossed in this wide world alone,
> no hope have I for tomorrow,
> I've started to make heaven my home.

> Sometimes I am tossed and driven, Lord
> Sometimes I don't know where to roam,
> I've heard of a city called heaven,
> I've started to make it my home.

> My mother has reached that pure glory,
> my father's still walkin' in sin,
> my brothers and sisters won't own me,
> because I am tryin' to get in.
>
> Sometimes I am tossed and driven, Lord
> Sometimes I don't know where to roam,
> I've heard of a city called heaven,
> I've started to make it my home.

The sorrow of being tossed in life is named but it appears that these circumstances cause the singer to start making heaven his or her home in the present, not just in the future. This approach of thinking about heaven now and not just later points to the double meaning of many spirituals, as already discussed in chapter 1.

There are different opinions about "heaven" in the spirituals. Some say it shows that "other-worldly hope looms large."[53] Others believe the metaphor of heaven is not escapist. Rather, it is a "principle of social criticism well camouflaged in the prominent Christian language of the day."[54] One does not have to choose sides, the historical or metaphysical perspective. One can hold on to the tension involved in singing of a heavenly home and envision heaven as both this-worldly and otherworldly, a land of concrete freedom with earthly relevance and a world beyond the final death. Hope, in this way, manifests itself in the present and future. Either way, one is a "heav'n boun' soldier." The imagery of heaven is critical for reimagining God's world. Arthur Jones, who stresses the earthly dimensions of heaven language, refers to the heavenly minded spiritual "I Got a Robe" and says this:

> This song is not about wishing to die and going to Heaven. Rather, it employs the imagery of Heaven, *in the imagination*, to construct a different definition of life in the present. It is a statement of the singer's confident knowledge that even though there are no earthly shoes (or other physical comforts) provided to slaves, everyone is worthy of shoes, and everyone is a child of God, despite external definitions to the contrary . . . the singer creates a new, here-and-now definition of the self.[55]

Spiritual preaching is fluid and adaptable in its expressions of hope, especially as it relates to heaven, home. Thus there are multiple meanings of heaven. Going home to heaven, whatever the perspective, generated hope for those who suffered greatly in the journey of life. What is important to note is that hope was a journey in the path of death. It was not stagnant but represented a desire for something more, something better for humanity. The journey expressed by these cultural musical sermons is instructive for contemporary preaching and the meaning of preaching in the Spirit as it relates to death and hope.

Preaching Death and Hope in the Spirit

There are several implications for preaching that are initiated by the previous conversation about death and hope in the Spirit(uals). I will discuss four of them in this section though there are other implications as well; thus what follows is not exhaustive but suggestive in nature. Yet, what should be evident is the "eternality of message"[56] embedded in the spirituals. Though contextually created and historically situated in a different time and space than today, the spirituals proclaim a timeless, universal message of struggle, pain, and hope. These human experiences cross cultures and traditions and span diverse spaces and time, revealing that the gospel travels and transgresses boundaries. There is not always a one-to-one correlation between the spiritual homiletical tradition and contemporary preaching because specific human needs vary, but there *are* needs nonetheless that preaching will hopefully meet by the grace and power of God.

People suffer from "little deaths" regardless of creed or color, space or time, yet hope is still expressed in many lives. Preaching in the Spirit, spiritual preaching, as discussed above, means that one faces death squarely with hope because the Spirit is present through proclamation in the valley of dry bones, in both the death experienced and hope expressed. The spirituals demonstrate this courageously and creatively as the Spirit speaks of death and hope together through these sermonic songs. The spirituals reveal that preaching does not avoid present struggle or a future home with God. One's homiletical feet are firmly planted in this world and another realm. The Spirit bridges the gap between these realities. Christian preachers minister at the intersection of a world of death and a world of hope. Both are true but how one conveys the relationship of death and hope in preaching will depend somewhat on how one's preaching sounds.

Sound the "Mood"

Preaching death and hope in the spiritual homiletical tradition possesses a certain soundscape. Acoustics and embodiment matter, not just words. This is true for the entire community in light of the antiphonal nature of many black preaching expressions. With this understanding of preaching, the "mood"[57] takes priority. *How* one talks about death and expresses hope is just as important as *what* one says about them. Spiritual sounds are an epistemological site for theological revelation, for speaking and hearing the death and hope of humanity and God. The ministry of preaching entails nurturing a sonic spirituality. Evans Crawford argues, "The sound of the sermon is not simply something added to the substance but rather is inseparable from the experience of participant proclamation."[58] But verbal, vocal, and physical gestures solely are insufficient for sounding the mood of preaching. To sound the mood, a preacher has to be *in* the mood. As I tell students, "You can't give what you ain't got." One will not be able to articulate suffering and hope authentically if one is detached from these realities and not invested in embodying them. To capture the mood orally/aurally, one has to know death, suffering, and hope for him- or herself. Empathy with the human condition is vital for any genuine voicing of the certain sound of spiritual preaching. Preachers are a "part of the human condition,"[59] thus, when one suffers, all should suffer and if one rejoices, all should rejoice (1 Cor. 12:26). Without empathic engagement with others, it will be difficult to get into the mood that is appropriate for preaching death and hope.

One should be totally invested in what one is saying because the spirituals as musical sermons "[are] written in [slaves'] blood."[60] Too many people have died for the gospel for contemporary preachers to be better comedians than proclaimers of Christ. Spiritual preaching requires sweat, blood, and tears because this kind of proclamation is costly, in that life and death are at stake. Because of the weightiness of the gospel and this age of death, there are no excuses for disinterested proclamation. Why preach if one is not in the mood? Without the mood, hearers will experience an incongruent word, a disconnection between what is said and how it is said. One's sermon form might be fluid, theology on target, hermeneutical approach to the text sophisticated and creative, introduction attention-grabbing, but if one does not vocalize and embody, that is, perform, the word appropriately to the weighty issues being proclaimed, one's preaching will fail, dying a slow death as the sermon dribbles down the front of the pulpit before it even reaches the ears of the congregation. Sounding the mood of death and hope requires intensified interaction of logos, pathos, and ethos.[61] The mood of spiritual preaching calls for holistic engagement. A deep feeling is necessary, more than any amount of artistic technique. Sounding the mood reveals that one believes what one says. If one sounds the mood, people will recognize that death is real and so is hope.

This homiletical sounding is so significant (though this has been traditionally marginalized in homiletical literature compared to the "real content of preaching") that it requires one's entire homiletical arsenal. The homiletical musicality that has already been discussed—repetition, rhythm, antiphony, melody, body, metaphoric coded language—conjoin the other basics of preaching to help voice the mood. It will be sonic and somatic because it is pneumatic. The preacher becomes the instrument such that the "preacher's voice is the full orchestra."[62] To "hear the word of the LORD," as Ezekiel says, suggests that the word of the Lord is sounded in order to be heard. The word is sense and sound.[63] Words alone cannot capture the depth and tragedy of death nor the heights of bliss and hope in the face of death. It may take groans and moans to preach the gospel and shouts of joy when there appears to be nothing to shout about. In terms of sermonic language, the words used should have feet and dance, standing upright like a glorious resurrection, moving and grooving to the rhythms of the Spirit of life, and not be so flat as to make a bed in some lonesome dry valley.

In other words, what has been seen with the coded, imagistic language in the spirituals is poetic speech. There were literal utterings of proclamation (e.g., "no more peck 'o corn for me") but also figurative ones that influence the sounding of the mood. Walter Brueggemann writes, "poetic speech is . . . the only proclamation . . . that is worthy of the name *preaching*" and such preaching is "the ready, steady, surprising proposal that the real world in which God invites us to live is not the one made available by the rulers of this age."[64] The language of "heaven," for instance, is an invitation to live in God's world and way. Other imagery such as the promised land, train, or sailing are poetic expressions used to speak of human and divine life. Poetic language has always been important in African American preaching historically. In *I Believe I'll Testify*, Cleo LaRue writes, "Blacks are taught early on to love words—to love how they *sound*, how they feel . . ."[65] Poetic language is critical to sounding the mood of death and hope. This love of language and aim for well-crafted speech is still important in many black churches. "Many blacks continue not only to dress themselves in their Sunday best for the worship service but also to dress their English in its Sunday best."[66] This linguistic dressing exemplifying "the will to adorn"[67] fosters a certain mood, whether in the preaching of death or hope. The free, creative, artful language of spiritual preaching renders God present, evoking awe and mystery of the divine.[68] Sound says something about the presence of the Spirit and invites the Spirit. It also gives voice to one's own soul and faith.

Faith in God

Faith in God is another critical factor in thinking about preaching death and hope in light of the Spirit(uals). Spiritual preaching implies a deep personal trust in God. The unknown, black-bard musical preachers said,

> Mah God is so high
> You can't get over him
> So wide
> You can't get around him
> So low
> You can't get under him
> You mus' go through the Lam'.

When facing death and desiring to preach hope, a big God must be present. James Earl Massey represents the spiritual homiletical tradition when he writes, "Preaching lives in the reality that God *is* . . ." The fact that God is does not dissolve earthly hardships. Massey continues, "[Real preaching] faces reality, things as they are—human pain, sickness, disease, sin, distresses, calamities, personal and social evil—but always with concern to face them in the light of God's reality, the history of God's mighty acts, God's promises, and God's offered help."[69] The context of death is not erased nor ignored but neither is God. God is viewed as a mighty sovereign who acts on behalf of the oppressed and hurting. God does something. God is believed to make ways out of no ways, even in the valley of dry bones. God acts and is experienced in the contours of one's life and preaching. According to Tom Long, "either God is present and active in our preaching, or we are poseurs and pathetic fools."[70] Not only would we be fools but our sermons would join the collective family of dry bones in Ezekiel's vision. Without God, one cannot handle death or even know

hope. Thus God should be at the center of preaching in the Spirit that proclaims death and hope.

God is central but *human* faith in God is also important. The starting point in the ministry of preaching is not solely God, but faith in God,
despite little deaths. If one does not believe in the presence of the divine,
then why does one preach? If there is no faith, why preach? How can
one even preach the gospel without faith? Faithless preaching is Godless
preaching. Spiritual preaching possesses a tenacious belief in God. This
faith is necessary when facing death and for proclaiming death. Without it,
death will kill preachers. With it, preaching will be empowered just as the
bards' creativity was "powered by religious belief."[71] Homileticians speak
about "putting God at the center of the sermon,"[72] but the black bards
challenge contemporary preachers not only to do that but to put God at
the center of their lives. Those spiritual preachers knew the God whom
they proclaimed. Nothing less is required of today's preachers who want
to engage death hopefully. Preachers should seek to know God and love
God unashamedly with their entire being, always desiring to be in touch
with God because "homiletics is always more than method."[73] Preaching
in the Spirit calls for the preacher to embrace God and nurture the faith
of the community in order that their relationship with God might deepen
and strengthen.

Faith in God can grow with the recognition that hope rests with the
presence of God. Hope rises because God is present. Hope is not something
that humans generate or create but God sparks.[74] Without God, there is no
hope. Godless preaching is hopeless preaching. Faith in God is the environment out of which hope grows. Preaching hope rests on the premise of
faith and relationship with God. Because of this relationship and the Spirit
in our hearts (Rom. 5:5), hope can live in and through preaching. Hope
comes because God cares. Remembering "God's overall performance and
promises in human history" fosters hope in the midst of death.[75] James
Harris testifies about his own upbringing, revealing the linkage between
hope and God. He says, "I was frustrated with the social conditions, but I
was never without hope, because I believed that God was real and powerful."[76] His voice is an echo of the spirituals and the lives of many Christian preachers throughout the world: "Without [God] I could do nothing,
without [God] I'd surely fail; without [God] I would be drifting, like a ship
without a sail."[77] But with God, nothing is impossible (Luke 1:37), not
even the triumph of hope.

Triumph of Hope

Spiritual preaching holds death and hope together because without the embrace of death, one cannot preach Christian hope effectively. However, the spirituals also demonstrate that despite this creative tension, the voice of hope sounds triumphantly eventually. This is not to say that one overlooks "tellin' like it is" about sin and brokenness in the world. Little deaths are real and at times appear more real than God. But what I am suggesting is that in God, hope cannot be squelched. Spiritual preaching says hope and God win. Death is the climate for hope and sometimes death is perceived as the only hope. Also, the spiritual musical sermons reveal that hope is stirred in and despite death, formed on the anvil of hell. Thus one cannot neglect the fact of death as the context of preaching, but in the Spirit, there is more than death. There is life breathing in existential valleys, declaring, "You shall live." Just as the Ezekiel passage demonstrates a movement from death to life and hope, hope should have the final sermonic climactic word. A "glory hallelujah!" should ring out with linguistic trumpets.

Of course, just as some spirituals focus solely on death or hope and do not intermingle the two, there are times that sermons may do the same. This is not a call for a rigid homiletical rule that commands every sermon to move in the same way. There are some who argue for a certain sermon structure as a means to preaching hope.[78] This is not my focus, though a sermon structure could be informed by this notion of the triumph of hope as seen in "Nobody Knows the Trouble I See," such that a sermon moves from death to hope in its form. What is more significant in light of this project is the interplay of death and hope with the aim of proclaiming robust Christian hope in the mode of the Spirit(uals). There is a mixed texture but hope has the last word because God will have the last word. Hope is not a theme of a sermon or a refrain that has to be used but it is at the heart of what it means to preach in a valley of dry bones. Spiritual preaching restores hope to those who have lost it. Paul Scott Wilson says it right: "Hope is the nature and tenor of the gospel, thus hope is the ultimate nature and tenor of each sermon."[79] If preaching is in the Spirit, then hope is its tenor, not happiness, prosperity, or optimism. Hope is distinct.

Hope does not say that the road of life will be smooth and straight because it is often rough and crooked, especially for the marginalized in society. The irony, however, as Peter Gomes reminds us, is that "in and through suffering . . . hope is made manifest."[80] Pain and suffering are fodder for hope. Nonetheless, with the help of God, hope will reign in the ruins of this world. Gomes warns against cheap hope and says, "Hope is not merely the optimistic view that somehow everything will turn out all right in the end if everyone just does as we do. Hope is the more rugged, the more muscular view that even if things don't turn out all right and aren't all right, we endure through and beyond the times that disappoint or threaten to destroy us."[81] Hope goes beyond death and transcends it even while taking it seriously. Since the Spirit(ual) preaches death *and* hope, preaching in the Spirit involves tackling death in all of its variety while still proclaiming hope in this world and the next.

This leads to what might be deemed an uneasy conversation about the language of heaven in contemporary preaching. The spirituals preach the realm of heaven with courage but for today's postmodern audience, speaking of heaven may seem out of date and out of touch with the *real* world. For many in the Western world, reality is what can be seen. The unseen is untouchable and unutterable. The unseen world is a mystery but this does not mean it is unreal. Homileticians have noted that eschatology, the study of the last things, including heaven, is an "often neglected dimension"[82] in contemporary preaching. If not neglected, it is at least muted. But for those in the spiritual homiletical tradition, proclaiming heaven as home was full of hope.

To preach in the Spirit includes preaching the hope of heaven for the present and future. Samuel Proctor argues that the "fragrance of eternity" is in our midst. "Immortality begins now," he says, and "eternity flows in the midst of time."[83] The eternity of God's time envelops our time. Though in the world, Proctor represents the spirituals sermonic tradition when he declares, "We should be aware of our real and abiding spiritual home."[84] Our ultimate home is not this world. Our time and space is only one side of the human story. There is a world beyond this world that impinges on this world and our lives. We are a "colony of heaven, and we have other connections."[85] This is why we pray the Lord's Prayer, "Your kingdom come, your will be done, on earth as it is in heaven" (Matt. 6:10). The way of heaven is to be the way of earth. Believing this makes a huge difference in our present living. The realm of God, stated in "heaven," therefore is not escapist but, rather, plunges one deeper into the baptized life of Jesus Christ, into a different way of living on earth as it is in heaven. "Heaven" can propel people forward with hope if we proclaim it with a sense of hope, if we actually believe in this realm of God.

Hope will triumph in our preaching if we proclaim heaven as God's world that transcends this world. Preaching heaven raises the standard of how we should live right now. As noted, "heaven" is double coded in the spirituals, thus pertaining to both now and later. Preaching heaven is a matter of faith and confession, not scientific proof. It is a matter of hope in God, that God has a future for us that has an impact on the present state of affairs. Proclaiming heaven suggests another world where all is put to right and justice prevails. Proclaiming heaven suggests that this world is faulty and frail and does not meet divine standards. Preaching heaven is a poetic approach to "envisioning"[86] God's realm as a means to helping others realize that there is more to human existence than meets the eye. Preaching consists of leading others toward what God wants all of creation to be.

Nothing is wrong with yearning for home with God, to live in God's world, heaven. Heaven is a place of justice, jubilation, and rest. Even on the gospel train toward that goal, the vision of heaven can shape the present because the "rich an' poor are dere," there is no "diff'rence in de fare," and there is "no second class aboard dis' train." Whatever one's perspective on the reality of heaven, spiritual preaching demonstrates how "heaven" is both a transcendent future and present. Divisions and forms of alienation are removed and people are in community with God and each other. The metaphor of heaven as a way of speaking of God's future for us helps preachers envision "the new creation . . . in the midst of a world of death" and enables "God's people to imagine alternatives to a world governed by the powers."[87] This happens amid the powers of death and destruction. Preaching heaven will "call forth a world that does not exist"[88] on earth, a world based on God's promises. The biblical imagery of heaven can nudge listeners to move in the direction of this home of God. That one even moves is itself a revelation of the ultimate triumph of hope.

Preaching as Pilgrimage

The motivation of heaven engenders hope now, but since heaven is fully experienced at the end of time, spiritual preaching sings of death and hope while on a journey home. The spiritual proclamation of death and hope is a pilgrimage because weekly, one continues to preach. To preach death and hope is an ongoing ministry. For now, death does not cease, thus hope needs to be voiced continually. One sermon does not suffice. It is a pilgrimage, never fully arriving at home until God sees fit. If one did arrive at home, there would be no need to hope. But until that day, preachers hopefully proclaim hope despite the perpetual death. The language of heaven reveals that our world is not yet what it should be and we have not yet arrived in God's heaven. There are glimpses of hope but the final consummation has not happened. Heaven as the present future of God implies that preaching is not stagnant but is a journey toward God. On the journey, preaching encounters death and proclaims it, and because preaching is a pilgrimage, hope lives on the journey, too, moving us forward to the day when we will "never tire" in "de manshans above."

In the meantime, it is important for preachers to realize that victory does not happen overnight or with one good sermon. Death may depress but eventually the Spirit will animate hope through speech. Patience in the journey of preaching is essential as we wait for God's promises to be fulfilled so the world can be made right. James Kay believes, "Promises always entail an outstanding future between their uttering and their fulfillment. As such, divine promises simultaneously proclaim that God has a future, that God is our ultimate future, and that the final shape of the human community 'in Christ,' 'in the Spirit,' and 'in love' is on its way."[89] There is a trajectory toward God's future and preaching should point toward that future with hope. Spiritual preaching maintains hope as its heartbeat because hope is at the core of the ministry of preaching. On the journey, one will experience ups and downs and see the struggles of local communities and the global society. A pilgrimage is not necessarily smooth sailing. It is a process with twists and turns just like life. But as a process, hope has many opportunities to be voiced and not severed because the Spirit cannot be stopped. Death is not eternal, but life is timeless. This should motivate a pilgrim preacher to stay on the path toward home.

This chapter has been its own journey in exploring how the Spirit is involved in death and hope as expressed in Ezekiel and the spirituals. Death and hope are joined in the presence of the Spirit and in that presence, the real preaching of hope happens. The Spirit speaks death and hope, challenging the sound, faith, and hope of any preacher on the pilgrimage to God. Though it is a journey with mountaintops and valleys, one can rest assure that the Spirit is present even in the valley of dry bones. But as Ezekiel shows, those bones do not remain dry forever. Through the inspiration of the Spirit in preaching, those bones connect and rise to new life. Preaching in the Spirit, spiritual preaching, faces death directly as part of proclaiming hope.

3

Prophesy to the Bones

Generating Hope through Preaching

Then he said to me, "Prophesy to these bones . . ."

—Ezek. 37:4

You may have all dis world, but give me Jesus.

—Traditional

During the 2008 primary and presidential elections, there was a lot of talk about hope, particularly from the eventual winner, Barack Obama, who infused his speeches with a rhetoric of hope. One of his books is titled *The Audacity of Hope* and his 2008 election website stated that it was "Powered by hope."[1] Regardless of one's political leanings, one would be hard pressed to disagree with President Obama's statement, "There has never been anything false about hope."[2] Hope is true and real, but it can be defined in various ways; thus what President Obama meant by hope may not be the same sentiment voiced in the spiritual homiletical tradition. Stating "hope" alone does not generate it, guarantee its presence, nor tell us about its nature.

Generating hope through preaching has to do with what is known as the sermon function, that is, what one hopes will occur in the lives of the hearers due to the sermon.[3] In other words, spiritual preaching desires for hope to be created in the listening congregation. One prophesies to bones with a purpose. One hopes for hope and, as should be evident already, there is nothing false about hope (and death) in the spiritual homiletical tradition. The spirituals will be our guide to discern how we approach generating hope through preaching as we delve biblically, theologically, and homiletically into those places to which those musical sermons point. Whereas I previously explored thinking about the Spirit, death, and hope *in* the spirituals, here I will discuss homiletical theology, theory, and practice *from* the spirituals, going beyond them for contemporary homiletical relevance.

Ezekiel and the Spoken Word

Some may think that it is too audacious to speak of generating hope through preaching, but Ezekiel reveals that preaching or prophesying, in this context of death, is commanded by God (37:7, 10). To speak of generating hope does not mean that finite preachers are the generator. Preachers do not control whether hope is actually created in the encounter of speaking and listening during the preaching event. Rather, hope is a gift from God the Spirit, the Animator, the Breath of hope. Ezekiel makes clear that the divine breath, spirit, stirs life in the valley of dry bones.

However, Ezekiel reveals the rich connection between word and spirit or prophecy and Spirit that is so prevalent in the Bible.[4] Ezekiel 37 emphasizes the images of death and the references to the Spirit but just as prominent is the action of prophesying (vv. 4, 7, 9, 10, 12). This is not coincidental, because the Spirit collaborates with spoken word to spark hope in the domain of death. Word and Spirit together bring hope out of the valley of dry bones. God uses divinely sanctioned human speech, not a tweet, for God's resurrection purposes. Preaching is "God's human speech"[5] because it declares, "Thus says the Lord God" (vv. 5, 9, 12), and not whatever the preaching prophet desires.

Yet, God uses fallible human words as a conduit of hope for a dying and dead people. The Spirit is the Resurrector, but preaching-prophesying-the spoken word appears to be the means toward that end. In God's hands, the spoken word is a ministry of life. This is why, when faced with dry bones lying in the valley, the Lord tells Ezekiel to "prophesy to these bones" (v. 4). God could have found other means for restoration or given other instructions, like to call the funeral-home director, but God calls Ezekiel to preach, to use words in the valley of death as a life-giving act with the aim of resurrection. The weight of preaching is implied here in that it is revealed as a matter of life and death. God calls Ezekiel to prophesy in a graveyard of bones, risking contamination and his life.

Despite the risks, following the call and obeying the divine command are shown to be worthwhile for the community because each time Ezekiel notes that he prophesied "as I had been commanded" (vv. 7, 10), transformation begins. In one case, "a noise, a rattling" (v. 7) starts and in another, "the breath came" (v. 10). Through the spoken word, life is generated. Even more radical is the notion that preaching is an invocation for the Spirit, the breath, to come as Ezekiel was told to "prophesy to the breath" (v. 9). Preaching ushers in breath. Pneumatic speech is an impetus to divine transformation in the domain of death. Preaching should not be taken lightly because words do things, as demonstrated in this passage.[6] In the power of the Spirit, when Ezekiel prophesies, something happens for the life of a community.

The truth is that a preacher does not know what the results of his or her spoken words will be. They can only say, like Ezekiel, "O Lord God, you know" (v. 1). Nonetheless, the call to proclaim comes on divine terms and preachers can only willingly say, "I'm gonna preach when the Spirit says-a preach." Furthermore, the fact that God still commands one to prophesy suggests that God has not given up on God's creation or preaching itself because preaching is a form of help from God.[7] Kenyatta Gilbert states that "in preaching, the hope of God speaks."[8] Thus God is not finished with us yet and still offers hope to the hopeless. God provides prophets and servants to be agents of hope in dying communities, contemporary graveyards. Words are used as nonviolent weapons to fight death and embody God's hope. Ezekiel demonstrates that the Spirit does not work alone in the valley of dry bones but partners with the spoken word in preaching for the divine purpose of generating life and hope. This biblical metaphor uses death to awaken us from our homiletical sleep in order to realize what is at stake when we preach in the valley of dry bones and to reclaim the importance of preaching today because when we preach in the Spirit, the possibility of hope is always present.

Embracing the Eschaton

The horizon of hope in preaching that Ezekiel reveals comes through clearly in the spirituals. These musical sermons imply that preachers should not fear the end, "the last things,"[9] because of a courageous vision of God's ultimate home and God's purposes for all of creation. Rather, the spirituals call preachers to embrace the eschaton. As noted already, scholars often say that eschatology is neglected in contemporary preaching, but in traditional African American preaching eschatological themes still play an important role. It is important to put "last things" first when thinking about generating hope in preaching because "how it ends affects the whole and implies the beginning."[10] One approaches the proclamation of hope with God's end in view. That ending, the fulfillment of God's good purposes for all of creation through a new creation, is the preacher's beginning. The prevalence of the images of heaven and other themes of the eschaton within the spirituals makes it difficult for preachers to ignore the end or "to roll up their windows and lock their doors while driving through the New Testament's eschatological neighborhoods."[11] Not solely the spirituals, but the Spirit, who is given to us by God (Rom. 5:5), would seem to make it impossible for us to neglect the end because the Spirit fosters "the experience of eschatological epistemology."[12] The Spirit helps us to know and experience a foretaste of God's future to come.

Spirit of Hope

Preaching in the Spirit must be hopeful in an eschatological way. It is not surprising that many spirituals sing of going home to heaven: "Goin' to put on my robe," "De angels in heab'n gwineter write my name," "Walk in Jerusalem jus' like John," or "Ride up in de chariot, soon-a in de mornin' an' I hope I'll jine de ban'." The spirituals stem from the Spirit, as I have argued, and the Spirit of the spirituals is an eschatological Spirit. As musical sermons of the Spirit, the spirituals are inherently linked to eschatology, the last things. A *spiritual* preacher could not avoid it even if she or he so desired. Even the vision of the Spirit in the valley of dry bones, the operative metaphor in this book, represents a Jewish idea that views the Spirit as key to Israel's eschatological future and restoration of a community.[13]

The Spirit nudges preachers to embrace the eschaton and is essential to the process of generating hope in others. James Dunn asserts that in Pauline thought "hope [is] one of the primary blessings of the Spirit."[14] Frequently, Paul correlates the Spirit and hope. In Romans 8, Paul presents the eschatological nature of the Spirit of hope through the image of groaning. In this scriptural setting, creation, humanity, and the Spirit, groan (vv. 22-23, 26), due to "the sufferings of this present time" (v. 18). Pain is present and acknowledged through the expression of groaning. Yet, these groans are not representative just of suffering but of a hope for a "glory about to be revealed" (v. 18), future redemption (vv. 23-25).

These hope-filled groans reveal the eschatological Spirit. For instance, the groaning voiced by believers who have the "first fruits of the Spirit" indicates a divine pledge that will eventually be fulfilled. The first fruits is a metaphor derived from giving the first fruits of crop to God in confidence that God will bring an abundant harvest. First fruits imply that there is a guarantee from God in the present about the final redemption.[15] Through the Spirit, a new age has begun but it has yet to be fully realized; this is known as the "already-not yet" eschatological tension of the Christian life. Thus there is still death and hope experienced in the present as we live "between what we are and what we shall be."[16]

This is the eschatological context of spiritual preaching. The groans continue until the full consummation of God's new age, but because these groans also suggest hope for the future and not just suffering, they indicate that there is more than death to this life. There is hope and, despite the groaning tension, the confident testimony is that "hope does not disappoint" (Rom. 5:5). Suffering and death will not say the benediction at the end of the service of life. Hope will declare it in the Spirit, perhaps even with a celebratory doxology (Rom. 8:39). Embracing the eschaton in preaching as a part of generating hope in others' lives may lead one and others to a mode of praise never experienced. Spirit(ual) preaching is inherently eschatological, thus doxological, not fearing God's end for the world as we know it, but anticipating it with courageous hope and worship.

This eschatological perspective situates preaching in its proper place as a ministry of hope in the Spirit of hope while in the midst of groaning realities of death. To embrace the end, the eschaton, is to embrace the one who is our beginning and end in faith, love, and hope. The eschaton as a homiletical lens may help put congregational problems into perspective because eschatology implies that God is not finished with us yet. The journey of life continues and we have not reached our home, what we shall be. The struggles and pains of life, the little deaths, are not the totality of human existence, though they may appear to be at times. A view toward the end could assist preachers to realize, as Martin Luther King Jr. said, "Death is not a period that ends the great sentence of life, but a comma that punctuates it to more lofty significance."[17] The eschaton tells us that life is eternal and death will eventually die. In the Spirit, one can know this with hope as one yearns for and works toward God's future in the present.

Future Present Hope

To embrace the eschaton in preaching does not mean one ignores the earth. Rather, spiritual preaching invites God's kingdom to come and will to be done "on earth as it is in heaven" in the present (Matt. 6:10). To generate hope in preaching, eschatology needs to be earthy—not just heavenly minded, but earthly good. The spirituals showed this dimension of eschatological nuance, particularly in relation to their "mask" or double meaning. Many of these musical sermons that spoke of crossing the Jordan or sweet chariots "comin' for to carry me home" were not necessarily just about traveling to heaven; they could also refer to happenings on the earth, secretly calling the enslaved to an earthly freedom. "Steal Away" is a classic example of hope in the present for the future:

> Steal away, steal away, steal away to Jesus!
> Steal away, steal away home, I ain't got long to stay here!
>
> My Lord calls me, He calls me by the thunder;
> The trumpet sounds within-a my soul, I ain't got long to stay here.

This spiritual could be about "stealing away" to the home known as heaven, but it also could be a call to "steal away" to a free, physical place or a secret meeting among the slaves. The hope voiced in this musical sermon is double-voiced; it is about another world *and* this world. This is informative for preaching today because within an eschatological horizon, there is hope in the present because of the future.

Embracing the eschaton in preaching does not mean that we proclaim "I'll fly away" as we wave goodbye to our neighbors in need. Rather, God's end shapes the direction in which humans move and work on the earth. Thus, through the Spirit, the future becomes present and the end is already though not yet fully realized. Dale Andrews states, "Black eschatology does not separate 'other-worldly' and 'this-worldly' hope . . . otherworldly promise translates into this-worldly hope and ways of being."[18] He states further, "Future expectations invoke responsibility for the present. Likewise, future hope sustains and empowers us in living in the present."[19] Hope can be generated not only because of a future eternal redemption but because of a present social redemption that is fashioned in the mode of God's future, even if it is a challenge to the present order of things. What is important for preaching that desires to generate hope is to be neither "crassly materialistic or hopelessly otherworldly."[20] One preaches within the tension of God's future present, knowing that "the full disclosure of God is not fully contained in the present tense."[21] Present-tense preaching reveals glimpses of God in the world and invites others to participate in this "hope-shaped mission"[22] that works toward God's restorative new creation for all things.

This grounded, earthy eschatology of a future present hope suggests that this hope is not naïve but "blues-inflicted" and "tear-stained."[23] Hope resides in the ruins of the everyday. Embracing the eschaton in this manner does not alleviate preachers from dealing with "de troubles of the world" but calls them and others to engage in the hard work that moves society toward God's future in the present. Generating hope in preaching means that one proclaims "freedom in a time of captivity, the gift of peace to a world of conflict, and joy even as the lamenting continues."[24] Prophesying to the dry bones is a vocalized and embodied "hope in the holler."[25] Future present hope does not negate the holler or hell of life. Ezekiel reveals that hope is born in a valley of dry bones. Embracing the eschaton as an avenue toward this *spiritual* homiletics of hope that aims to generate hope is only one critical theme to which the spirituals point. The other vital prominent theological theme found in the spirituals and critical to generating hope is Jesus Christ.

Proclaiming Jesus

The eschatological images within the spirituals are obvious and it is also impossible to ignore the christological ones as well. As James Weldon Johnson notes in his preface to *God's Trombones,* slave preachers instilled in black peoples "the narcotic doctrine epitomized in the Spiritual, 'You May Have All Dis World, But Give Me Jesus.'"[26] What preachers preached, the spirituals also proclaimed—Jesus. The exodus narrative and the future kingdom of God were important for the enslaved, but the focus on Jesus that reverberates in the cultural historical corridors is unavoidable. The spirituals point preachers toward the christocentric nature of generating hope. As songs of the Spirit, the spirituals not only emphasize eschatology but also Christology because the Spirit is "indivisibly bound"[27] to the total history of Christ. Spiritual preaching generates hope by proclaiming Jesus. Jürgen Moltmann writes, "The experience of the Spirit is never without the remembrance of Christ, never without the expectation of his future.[28] In the Spirit, the past, present, and future of Jesus are the homiletical hub of hope. To attempt to preach Christian hope without preaching Jesus is misguided. But the spirituals do not highlight a triumphalistic, militaristic, imperialistic Christ. Rather, they lead the way in proclaiming Jesus in such a manner that does not make him a "superman."[29] Instead, these cultural musical sermons reveal that the way of hope is via the way of death, the death of Jesus.

Were You There? Death of Jesus

A survey of the spirituals will show that the Jesus most highlighted in these musical sermons is a suffering Jesus. Death permeates the images of Jesus in these proclamatory songs. There are spirituals about his birth and resurrection but it is his death that is central. His death is the hope. The spiritual preachers sang, "Were you there when they crucified my Lord? Were you there when they nailed him to the tree? Were you there when they pierced him in the side? Were you there when the sun refused to shine? Were you there when they laid him in the tomb?" At other times, they sang,

> Calvary, Calvary, Calvary, Calvary,
> Calvary, Calvary, Surely he died on Calvary.
>
> Don't you hear the hammer ringing?
> Don't you hear the hammer ringing?
> Don't you hear the hammer ringing?
> Surely he died on Calvary.

Through lyrical and musical repetition and amplification, the hearer has to pay attention to "Calvary" and "the hammer ringing." Calvary, the place of the death of Jesus, was in fact a place of hope for the singing preachers and hearers because there was the belief that "Jesus suffers with us."[30] Humanity is not alone in its suffering and death. God works in the midst of death and is not afraid of death. Those suffering identify with Jesus' suffering and can find solace and hope in it. Spiritual preaching does not fear blood and death because the heart of Jesus is cruciform. The cross is fused with the lynching tree, the electric chair, and other forms of torture such that James Cone comments, "the lynched black victim experienced the same fate as the crucified Christ."[31]

Proclaiming Jesus means that Jesus was on death row, a crucified lockdown. "They crucified my Lord an' He nevuh said a mumbalin' word."

Spiritual preachers are not afraid to tell the story of Christ's death. To generate hope in preaching, one has to tell the truth about God. The truth is that Jesus wept, suffered, and eventually died like a common criminal. This is the gory gospel truth.

> Jesus, my darling Jesus,
> Groaning as the Roman spear plunged in his side;
> Jesus, my darling Jesus,
> Groaning as the blood came spurting from his wound.
> Oh, look how they done my Jesus.[32]

This raw gospel of God does not make sense to many. It is considered foolishness (1 Cor. 1:18). Yet, there is wisdom in knowing that suffering and death are not ends in themselves, where Jesus, the crucified Christ is concerned. Redemption will rise from human ruins, thus preaching Jesus' death is vital to future redemption. Spiritual preaching proclaims a *crucified* Messiah, "a lamb standing as if it had been slaughtered" (Rev. 5:6), one ruling not by military might but by love. His death shows strength, not weakness. It represents hope, not hell or something humorous. To "take it to the cross" in black preaching does not mean one celebrates death and violence, but one celebrates a love that is faithful unto death, showing great mercy, and giving free grace. One celebrates a love that is stronger than death, even the death of death, which is the birth of hope. "What Christians celebrate is that death and evil do not have the final victory; the power of God does."[33] To proclaim "Christ crucified" (1 Cor. 1:18, 23-24) is to proclaim the power of God, not the weakness or death of God. The full story of the death of Jesus includes life. That is the hope in death, or death as the hope, which permeates spiritual preaching.

Elsewhere, I call the death of Jesus a "death threat" to death.[34] Spiritual preaching proclaims this death and aims to generate hope through it. All of this suggests that the image of the Lamb is important in proclaiming Jesus because that biblical image implies death and the cross. But through his death and bloody fleece, death is no more. One spiritual that points in this direction preaches, "O de Lamb done been down here an' died / Sinner won't die no mo'." Through one death, there is "no mo'" death ultimately. Preaching Jesus to generate hope has to embrace the death of Jesus to embrace the hope found in him. In fact, death by itself is insufficient because "the cross was not the end of God's drama of salvation. Death does not have the last word. Through Jesus's death, God has conquered death's power over his people."[35] In the end, there is hope and life. James Kay revisits the Apostles' Creed's phrase, "He descended into hell," and asserts, "If death were an impenetrable barrier for God's redeeming grace, then death would be God. Death would have the final word, and death would have the final victory over life. Christ's descent into hell, as descent to the dead, disputes this claim of death to absolute lordship."[36] Jesus infiltrates death's headquarters to destroy death once and for all. God's power is revealed through suffering love, death. God enters the depths of creation's suffering in order to redeem it for life. Because Jesus "'made it' to hell and back," there is nothing and no one who is beyond the reach of God's love and grace.[37] Hope rises from death's domain. Ain't dat good news?!

To get to the possibility of good news, one has to face the bad news, the death, first. One has to face the wounds of Jesus and proclaim Jesus, all of the history of Jesus Christ. The spirituals stress the death of Jesus quite clearly and there is hope found through his death. But this is not to say that there are not other depictions of Jesus. However, spiritual preaching puts a greater emphasis on the death of Jesus, especially if one takes seriously the valley of dry bones and the reality of little deaths. Preaching Jesus is not prosperity preaching because the "bitter pill" of preaching is that the cross is "wrapped around the resurrection."[38] Surely he died on Calvary. Were you there?

Many are there due to contemporary crucifixions and not just those crucifixes hanging around one's neck. Preachers need to be there in order for their preaching to take us there, to Jesus. If sermons do not proclaim Jesus, they will go nowhere. As the spiritual says, preachers "mus' come in by an through de Lam'." Access to God is via dying. A preacher can "take it to the cross," which normally refers to what happens at the end of a sermon in a climactic, celebratory manner. But taking it to the cross is not just about the cross but implies the resurrection and the empty tomb. Cleo LaRue notes that "if you simply detail the events surrounding the death of Jesus you have not given a full account of God's ultimate redeeming act. . . . It is true that many black sermons end with the sweet moan of the black preacher crying out, 'He died on Calvary, yes he did.' But the good news is not complete until the preacher also proclaims, 'But early, early on the third day morning God raised him from the dead . . .'"[39] Therefore, proclaiming Jesus to generate hope is not just about dying, though that is a significant aspect of it; it is also about rising and living into a divine hope and promise.

He 'Rose: Hope in Jesus

The death of Christ was not the end of the Spirit's story, thus it is not the end of spiritual preaching. The spiritual homiletical tradition also proclaims, "He 'rose, He 'rose, He 'rose from the dead, An' de Lord shall bear my spirit home." Though it may have a different tone than the death-centered spirituals, these musical sermons still preach Jesus, the living crucified one. The death of Jesus is not forgotten because "They crucified my savior . . . [but] He 'rose." The spirituals lead us to hope through the resurrection as well. Jesus is not hanging on the lynching tree any longer nor is he in the tomb. The tomb is still empty and his body still cannot be found. From this perspective, emptiness is a source of hope and joy. Preaching the empty tomb is a call for hopeless, fearful weeping to cease: "Weep no more, Marta, Weep no more, Mary, Jesus rise from de dead, Happy Morning."

God swallows up the death of hope through the resurrection. Preaching that Jesus rose and lives is preaching that hope lives today. Spiritual preaching has to proclaim a living Jesus because the source of this preaching, the Spirit, is the one who raises him from the dead (Rom. 8:11). Raising the dead is an eschatological symbol, thus through the resurrection of Christ, we receive a pledge of God's promised future and a foretaste of the new creation. Proclaiming Jesus generates hope and is itself eschatological in nature, thus another form of embracing the eschaton. The Spirit urges preaching to mediate suffering and hope in the present, even as we anticipate the future in him. Preaching Jesus does not just contain the bad news of death but it transforms this death into the good news of eternal life via the resurrection that happened "early in de mornin', Hallelujah!"

In *Naming Grace,* Mary Catherine Hilkert writes about the significance of the paschal imagination and states that the "hope of the paschal imagination is that death, injustice, and loss do not have the final word; the future lies in the hands of the living God."[40] This is certainly a reason for "Hallelujah!" Proclaiming Jesus generates hope through this voice of courageous praise. Preachers can praise because of the ultimate dismantling of the powers that oppress and depress. David Buttrick asserts, "The resurrection declares that God is greater than militarism, economic greed, power politics, and yes, even greater than our ecclesial loyalties. All these powers, according to the Bible, will be put in their place by the risen Lord Jesus Christ (1 Cor. 15:24-28)."[41] These powers of death become impotent in the arms of a resurrected Jesus. In other words, "Death's sting is in the very life of God, overcome in the cross and resurrection of Jesus. God swallowed up death in victory. In the words of Jürgen Moltmann, 'Death will die, not-being will be no longer, hell will go to hell.'"[42] Spiritual preaching has to be bold because of the domain of death in which it proclaims. Preaching Jesus is not for the fainthearted or faithless. It is for those who desire to generate hope in the lives of people, many of whom may be on their spiritual deathbed. The resurrection of Jesus reassures us of the eternal hope that can be experienced today and it reminds us that life and death are in the balance.

Spiritual preaching is a serious ministry that should not be taken lightly. It is weighty and its pressure is felt in the world by the grace of God. The empty grave is an opening into future possibilities for humanity and creation. The stone has been rolled away from human existence such that no one has to be enclosed in darkness and fear. The light of a new day shines on humanity because of the work of God through Jesus Christ. This miraculous work demonstrates that the grave is not a dead end. Rather, it is the beginning of a new life and resuscitation of real hope that breaks into the present. N. T. Wright argues that it is significant that the resurrection happened "within our own world," thus its effects should be felt in our world.[43] This means that proclaiming Jesus is not a philosophical concept or the most recent speculative homiletical theory. It means that proclaiming Jesus to generate hope is grounded in this world and should have an impact on this world. The resurrection touches the earth and challenges the mission of the church to anticipate God's future purposes through concrete action in the direction of God's future.[44] This means that the church will be a "constant disturbance in human society."[45] Preaching Jesus is proclaiming all of who Jesus is and what Jesus did, his life and work, such that our preaching of hope in him guides our service through him in the world. In this way, hope becomes enfleshed in society.

In addition, to proclaim Jesus and the hope of the resurrection does not imply that preachers should preach about the resurrection every week. Rather, through the Spirit the essence of preaching possesses resurrection power even if one never explicitly speaks about the resurrection. Richard Lischer calls this "resurrection preaching by which the life of the risen Christ is made accessible to those who are dying in sin and despair."[46] Even without preaching the resurrection, preaching still "bears in its own fiber a note of victory."[47] Through spiritual preaching, the Spirit of the resurrection causes others to rise through mere human words.

It should now be clear that hope is generated by preaching the death and resurrection of Jesus because Christian hope is founded on Jesus Christ. To proclaim Jesus, the death of him and the hope in him, does not mean that every sermon has to say "Jesus" or literally "take it to the cross" and empty tomb. The sermon by itself should not carry this responsibility on its own every week. Ideally, the larger liturgical setting of corporate worship would also proclaim Jesus in word and action, thus relieving the preaching moment from bearing the burden of being the only liturgical act that would ever speak of Jesus. Saying this, however, does not relieve preachers from declaring the gracious promises of God on a weekly basis.

In light of the spiritual homiletical tradition, these divine promises are most effectively proclaimed when one preaches Jesus. This is inescapable in spiritual preaching and hope in Jesus does not negate or forget the death of Jesus. They exist in tension, an eschatological one, which prevents preaching from becoming triumphalistic because "we live the resurrection by carrying a cross."[48] "He 'rose" but the spirituals also challenge us not to forget that he died. At the heart of the eschatological vision is this christological vein that weaves itself through the spiritual musical sermons. Christian hope is linked to the *entire* history of Jesus Christ. Christian eschatology is grounded in the Christ event. The end has to do with the one who is the beginning and the end, Alpha and Omega, Jesus himself (Rev. 22:13). Spiritual preaching is unashamed of a christocentric gospel (Rom. 1:16) that preaches the dying of Jesus and his rising because "if Christ has not been raised from death, then we have nothing to preach and you have nothing to believe" (1 Cor. 15:14). Proclaiming Jesus reveals that one is a "prisoner of hope."[49] As preaching prisoners, we continue to hope "until he comes" (1 Cor. 11:26).

Preaching Practice

The larger theological framework of embracing the eschaton and proclaiming Jesus can be partnered with specific homiletical approaches in the hope of generating hope in the valley of dry bones. In homiletical terms, this hope can be expressed or yearned for through concrete forms when we practice preaching with the goal of generating hope in others. Hope is not purely a theological or philosophical ideal; it is an experiential phenomenon that may be initiated through homiletical means (and, of course, the work of the Spirit). To generate hope through preaching, the spirituals reveal that embracing the eschaton and proclaiming Jesus are critical. As shown, these two important theological themes are prominent in this cultural homiletical tradition and are helpful in framing what is required theologically in the proclamation of Christian hope. To go one step further, however, one should consider how one may generate hope through the actual practice of preaching. This section explores some pragmatic ways to move toward igniting hope in hearers.

The spirituals are also useful in this regard in that they are not just deeply theological and biblical sermons but rhetorically sophisticated. How these musical sermons are preached, the form in which they take shape, has an impact on how they are received. This is why acoustics are important when studying the spirituals and not just lyrics. The rhetorical makeup of the spirituals, including repetition, rhythm, antiphony, and melody, provide shape and sound to the theo-biblical content of their proclamation. The spirituals demonstrate not only the role of theology in generating hope but the significant impact of rhetoric in doing so. The spirituals lead me to explore some of the rhetorical means for generating hope, even as I go beyond the rhetoric of the spirituals to deepen the discussion about contemporary preaching.

There are at least three homiletical approaches that can foster an ignition of hope in other people. Before discussing those, it is important to highlight the fact that preaching, like singing, is itself a sign of hope, even before anything hopeful is declared. Preaching is a sign that God still loves the world enough to speak life and hope to it through human beings. It is a sign that God has not given up on God's creation and continues to beckon us to come. God so loved the world that God keeps revealing the word through preaching. Just as Pauli Murray has said, "Hope is a song in a weary throat,"[50] preaching is a song of hope echoing from weary preachers. As a song, preaching sounds the mood of the Spirit(ual), as noted in the previous chapter, which suggests that there is a certain sound that indicates hope. There is a certain rhetoric that aids in generating hope. "Hope" does not have to be literally voiced but it is "the ultimate nature and tenor of each sermon."[51] Nevertheless, one needs to consider how to generate hope through the rhetorical landscape of a sermon.

Preaching (within) the Tension

The first homiletical approach to generating hope is to preach the tension between death and hope. As I have said already, if there is no death, there can be no hope. One observes this with the history of Christ, and in the spirituals as well. In spiritual preaching, there is always a clear acknowledgment of the reality of little deaths. "Nobody knows the trouble I see" or "I know that water is chilly and cold," but these pronouncements about death's existence are met immediately with hope's determination expressed in words like "Glory, Hallelujah!" or "Hallelujah to dat Lam.'" The verses of "Balm in Gilead" represent a prime example of preaching the tension; for instance:

> If you cannot preach like Peter
> If you cannot pray like Paul,
> You can tell the love of Jesus,
> And say "He died for all."

Human shortcomings and frailty are articulated but the bright opportunity is also proclaimed. It is true that there is the ultimate triumph of hope in spiritual preaching, but there is nothing to triumph over if suffering, pain, and death are not preached, too. Though it may be tempting to only speak good news, the presence of bad news with the good news actually fosters an experience of the hope of the gospel.

To approach preaching this way is an embrace of the eschaton, the already-not yet tension of the Christian life. There is some "already" good news but there is also a lot of "not yet" despair and death. Even the eschaton of God includes both a promise and a judgment. Buttrick argues that this tension is important for the establishment of presence in preaching. He writes, "Phenomenologically speaking, presence is created by a sweet collision of past memory and future expectation."[52] As preachers proclaim the reality of little deaths while proclaiming another future present reality, the presence of hope can be generated. Present death is proclaimed boldly and the future of God is declared courageously because at their intersection, in this liminal space, hope lives. Buttrick says, "Only by preaching the future of God can a sense of God's presence once more fill the land," yet, "Too much heaven can cause a careless neglect of earthly affairs."[53] He understands the tension within spiritual preaching.

There are scholars who stress the tensive nature of the gospel and argue for a certain sermon movement in light of this tension. Thus, one half, the first half, of the sermon would deal with death and the latter half would point to life in God.[54] This is one possibility, but for my purposes what is more important than a particular sermon movement is for sermons to abide in the tension with the recognition that preaching in the Spirit "correlates with the ups and downs of life."[55] Sometimes we are down. Sometimes we are up. There are pockets of trouble and pockets of hope in society. A sermon in the spirituals mode maintains this tension as the heart of the gospel, a slaying-saving word.

When Gardner Taylor preaches "Betrayal," he takes the idea of "Friend" and utilizes it both as a reference to a little death of a broken relationship due to Judas's betrayal of Jesus and as a hopeful indication of God's eternal friendship toward us. He declares,

> Judas wrote his name in eternal shame. I have never known a parent to name a child "Judas." . . . How this act of treachery must have cut the heart of Jesus, but how often have we His people bruised and wounded Him anew. . . . The betrayer turns over his Lord to His enemies. . . . There is nothing on earth that hurts and embitters like that. My friend!

> Jesus looks at him. He looks at you and me. . . . Jesus says, "Friend, wherefore art thou come?" Well might He have asked, "Is it for this you have come?" "Friend!" as if to make one last appeal. "Friend, I am still on your side." Jesus says to Judas, "Friend." As if to say, "Have I ever failed you?" He flashed on Judas the majesty and sacredness against which Judas is now turned . . .

> He says to you and me as He implied to Judas: "Friend, have you ever called me and I did not answer? Friend, have I not stood with you?" We would have to answer, "What a Friend we have in Jesus, all our sins and griefs to bear."[56]

The irony in this sermon is that Jesus calls Judas and us "Friend" despite the betrayal and lack of friendship shown to him. In that one word is both the promise of God's infinite friendship extended toward humanity and the judgment of how humans can be Judas-like in that friendships can be often betrayed. Both perspectives are the gospel truth. Taylor preaches the tension of the Christian life, but he, like the spirituals, believes that hope triumphs, thus he ends by hymnically accentuating the friendship of God with "What a Friend We Have in Jesus."

Spiritual preaching does not avoid human struggle and frailty as expressed in such experiences like betrayal. However, often the final word of a sermon will voice the good news of God in an attempt to be sure that the listeners will be left at a point of hope. Some refer to this as the "but" in preaching. William McClain writes, "No matter how dark a picture has been painted or how gloomy, there is always a 'but' or a 'nevertheless' or an element in the climax of the sermon that suggests holding on, marching forward, going through, or overcoming."[57] It is this element of hope that rings out even as it "grows in distressful and muddy circumstances."[58] Hope grows out of the mud of death, keeping it honest and connected to the earth, while expressing the reality of a brighter future tasted in the present. This is hope on a homiletical tightrope.[59] The tightrope represents the balanced tension preachers must proclaim for the gospel to be heard in its fullest. Spiritual preaching operates most effectively in this tension because, just as resurrection preaching does, "it takes death seriously, denying neither death nor the alienation, loneliness, anxiety, sin and evil which cluster around it."[60] Yet, in the end, spiritual preaching, though surrounded by death, is not afraid to proclaim death's death. It takes courage and vision because until the end of all time, the tension will remain. The tension will not cease until sorrow and mourning are no more. Tension will not disappear until death dies. There is no resolution until the day of God's jubilee. Thus it is essential for preachers to preach the tension of death and hope but to do so with a *spiritual* vision. If not, hope will remain unborn.

Preaching (with) a Vision

A second homiletical approach to generating hope is to preach a vision. In other words, "Preacher, what do you see?"[61] In the midst of death, the unknown black bards saw God at work, even if at times it was only God's future work in another heavenly realm. Nonetheless, they possessed the "gift of seeing" and that enabled them to say some things that created hope in the hearers. Lischer, in his study of the preaching of Martin Luther King Jr., says, "The most fundamental characteristic of the poet is the gift of seeing one thing in terms of another or of seeing a greater reality hidden in the squalor of the everyday."[62] The unknown black bards were poetic prophets who saw beyond their circumstances. Little deaths could not defeat them as they envisioned "God's heab'n."

> I got a robe, you got a robe
> All o' God's chillun got a robe.
> When I get to heab'n
> I'm goin' to put on my robe
> I'm goin' to shout all ovah God's heab'n . . .

> I got a wings, you got a wings
> All o'God's chillun got a wings.
> When I get to heab'n
> I'm goin' to put on my wings
> I'm goin' to fly all ovah God's heab'n. . . .

This vision of heaven put the enslaved on an equal plane with those who oppressed them. In God's world, "all o'God's chillun" had robes and wings. They sensed another reality in the midst of their reality and this vision propelled them forward with courage and hope. They saw what many could not see and the world they saw was an indictment against the present world order. They envisioned a gospel train in which "de fare is cheap an' all can go, de rich an' poor are dere, no second class aboard dis train, no diff'rence in de fare." As they preached musically, they put forth a different vision than death's vision for them. Even when they wore the "mask," they proclaimed "God's a-gonna trouble de water." They cast a vision of freedom and preached the "ought-ness" of life rather than the "is-ness" of it. By preaching a vision of what ought to be, they were able to generate hope.

Spiritual preaching affirms "over my head I hear music in the air, there must be a God somewhere." If a preacher sees the hidden reality of God and is able to paint the picture of God's way and world, this will lead to hope in the listening audience. Chuck Campbell reminds us, "Hope is always hope in 'things not seen,' hope in the midst of a world in which the visions are not yet the full reality."[63] Though the vision is not full reality, it is still real(ity). Without a vision, preachers and their congregrants will perish. But painting a vision, creating a new world through language, allows others the opportunity to experience that vision in the present world. Fundamentally, this type of preaching indicates that "the future is not a void."[64] In a baccalaureate sermon titled "Tracks of My Tears," based on Revelation 5, I tried to follow the lead of the spirituals by preaching a vision that even this particular doxological pericope embodied. At the end of the sermon, I close with a climactic vision of inclusion of all of the constituencies mentioned earlier in the sermon:

> I hear John singing but he's not alone. I hear Oprah Winfrey, Barack Obama, Bill Gates, Martha Stewart, Donald Trump, Simon Cowell, Paula Abdul, Beyoncé, P. Diddy, fathers, mothers, husbands, wives, sons, daughters, Calvin, Luther, Barth, King, Cone, Cannon, Wall Street, and even the U.S. government. No one is left out of this hymn

sing. I hear Dan Migliore, Guy Hanson, Chuck Bartow, Don Capps, Abigail Evans, Randy Nichols, and all of us. I hear the birds in the air chirping. The cows in the field mooing. The dogs in the neighborhood barking. The cats down on Nassau Street meowing. "Every creature in heaven and on earth and under the earth and in the sea, all that is in them," singing not "me, myself, and I" but "To the one seated on the throne and to the Lamb be blessing and honor and glory and might forever and ever!" Amen! Amen! The future is God's and don't you forget it![65]

In this sermonic spiritual vision, "no one is left out of this hymn sing," even those one might not expect to be present at God's throne. It is a vision beyond the earthly norm, seeing what is not yet fully seen with human eyes. This is only one example of preaching a vision. In this case, it is of God's future for God's creation.

However, preaching a vision is not solely a grand cosmic perspective on God's future world; it is also grounded on earth where one sees glimpses of God's kingdom already breaking into this world. It is a future present hope. A proclaimed vision does not only include pictures or images of God's future but entails naming God's presence in today's world. Some call these glimpses "tokens of the resurrection."[66] J. Alfred Smith's statement that "Hope is a tiny sprout growing in cracked concrete"[67] is informative because hope may just be a small sprout in a vast context of cracked reality. Because of this, a preacher's spiritual sight needs to be highly sensitive, paying attention to God's presence in the world and naming it for the hearers. By doing so, preachers help others realize "hope as present"[68] on the earth and not locked in a heavenly home. The double coded nature of many spirituals suggests hope as present, at least in a subtextual reading of the spirituals. For instance, "Steal Away" has to do with God's liberating action in this world through physical escape and not just another future world. To preach a vision, sometimes one has to search for the "tiny sprout" in the domain of death.

In March, 2000, horrendous floods hit Mozambique, leaving many homes and lives threatened and lost. It was a sea of death literally. One woman, Ms. Pedro, climbed into a tree for safety and shelter once the floods overwhelmed her home. She was in the tree for three days. Some of her relatives, including her grandmother, were killed in the floods. Near the end of her time in the tree, she gave birth to a daughter.[69] Life was born in the midst of death. An African tree became a contemporary tree of life. Crying could be heard from those dying in the floods, but life and hope, in the form of a newborn baby, was crying, too. Howard Thurman was so right to write, "All around us life is dying and life is being born." The birth of this child in a tree was "life's most dramatic answer to death," "the Growing Edge incarnate."[70] A preacher should be able not only to see the tension of life/death in this scene but to see and proclaim "the growing edge" of the hope of God embodied in the little baby, a hope for the future of humanity. But one has to see glimpses of God's kingdom in order to say it in the pulpit. "Preaching eschatologically, therefore, points not to unassailable evidence of God's reign, but to fleeting signs and wonders, ambiguous glimpses of what shall surely be already spring, like green shoots in the desert, a word from God's future that reshapes our imaginations."[71]

Seeing God's presence in the world is vital to visionary preaching but one may also consider the necessary sense of hearing in relation to preaching a vision. Mary Catherine Hilkert argues that we can hear an "echo of the gospel" in the world if we have a sacramental imagination.[72] Thus the question to preachers is not just "What do you see?" but "What do you hear?" Preachers may be attuned to the sounds of the world and this may be true for those in the pews as well, but those in the pews are particularly attuned to the sounds of one's sermon, that is, sermon language. Sermon language shapes not only what one hears in the world but what one sees in the world. Therefore, sermonic language is linked to preaching a vision.

In Martin Luther King Jr.'s "strategy of elevation," Lischer observes that "rhetorical pleasure . . . can exalt the spirit and *create hope* where none has a right to exist."[73] Rhetoric is intertwined with the generation of hope. Preachers may be deemed "pulpit poets" who "image a world."[74] Preachers proclaim a vision of the kingdom of God but they also open a door into it, helping others live into this vision. Sermons could be thought of as a form of verbal iconography. In approaching the proclamation of a vision, mere prose is insufficient but metaphor is essential because "any approach to the mystery of God will be metaphorical."[75] Metaphor is critical to our language about God because no one has seen God, thus all our language about God is metaphorical in many ways. Spiritual preaching does not lock God in literalism as if God's nature or work in creation can be confined. Rather, it reaches for God and God's presence through metaphor. Metaphor in preaching is a prayer, a prayer that invites "the Holy Spirit to inspire faith and action."[76] It creates space for a vision to be imaged and lived into.

Linda Clader defines metaphor as "a linguistic phenomenon in which two words or concepts are juxtaposed to create a tensive relationship."[77] The most prominent metaphor in the spiritual homiletical tradition is the exodus.

> When Israel was in Egypt's land: Let my people go!
> Oppressed so hard they could not stand, Let my people go.
>
> Go down Moses, 'Way down in Egypt land,
> Tell ole Pharaoh, Let my people go.
>
> "Thus saith the Lord," bold Moses said, Let my people go;
> "If not, I'll smite your firstborn dead," Let my people go.
>
> Go down Moses, 'Way down in Egypt land,
> Tell ole Pharaoh, Let my people go.

In this case, historically, blacks saw the United States as Egypt while many whites saw the United States as the new Israel. For the enslaved, Pharaoh was the slave driver but they were Israel, the children of God, whom God was going to deliver out of Egyptian slavery. The use of this metaphor in this manner contradicted any notion that the United States was the promised land and "encouraged confidence among African Americans that change was possible in this world, not just in the next, and so enabled black people to hope, and when possible, to act."[78] This specific musical sermon paints a picture of a vision in which God has a Moses tell the oppressors "Let my people go." The biblical past became present in the sacred moment of song and preaching, instilling in the hearers the notion that God could still make a way out of no way and would "be wid us to the end."

This particular metaphor also reveals itself in the conclusion of King's final sermon.

> Like anybody, I would like to live a long life. Longevity has its place. But I'm not concerned about that now. I want to do God's will. And He's allowed me to go up to the mountain. And I've looked over. And I've seen the promised land. I may not get there with you. But I want you to know tonight, that we, as a people will get to the promised land. And I'm happy tonight. I'm not worried about anything. I'm

not fearing any man. Mine eyes have seen the glory of the coming of the Lord.[79]

King focuses on the promised land but this land is a part of the exodus motif, though it stresses the place of freedom and hope rather than the context of bondage. Nonetheless, King uses this historical cultural metaphor to create a vision and a hope for the future. The use of metaphor is not the only aspect of sermon language that fosters visionary preaching.

I have highlighted metaphor but other figures of speech such as hyperbole may be useful in preaching a vision as well. The writer/preacher of Isaiah engages in this when he says, "The wolf shall live with the lamb, the leopard shall lie down with the kid, the calf and the lion and the fatling together, and a little child shall lead them . . ." (Isa. 11:6-9). In addition, the use of repetitive sounds can be a helpful means for engaging a rhetoric of excess that signals the immensity or size of a vision. One old-time preacher, after closing the Bible, declares, "Brothers and Sisters, this morning I intend to explain the unexplainable—find out the undefinable—ponder over the imponderable—and unscrew the inscrutable."[80] This exaggerated, poetic-heightened language helps the listener to know that what he is about to talk about is bigger or grander than a normal coffee-shop conversation. Through his poetic repetition, the preacher signals that he is about to talk about God and when one speaks of God it has to be visionary and buoyant in nature. It has to be more than flattened prose.[81] Generating hope by preaching a vision requires the "will to adorn"[82] through metaphor and other linguistic means.

Preaching a Present God

Beyond preaching the tension and a vision, one who desires to generate hope in the hearers must certainly proclaim God. This is a third possible homiletical approach that follows the lead of the spirituals. The previous chapter already stated the importance of having faith in God as represented in the spiritual homiletical tradition. However, though many preachers possess faith in God, it does not mean that they proclaim God in the pulpit as a means of igniting hope in others. Some scholars would say that God is missing in many sermons, thus they make concrete suggestions to make God the literal subject of sermon sentences.[83] My intention here is not to suggest how to construct sentences but it is to affirm the necessity of offering God through preaching to the hearers as a path toward hope. Fundamentally, without God, there is no hope. God is the source of our hope (Psalm 62) because "hope is anchored in the Lord."[84] Hopeful spiritual preaching has its roots in God.

> The earth his footstool an' heav'n his throne,
> The whole creation all His own,
> His love an' power will prevail,
> His promises will never fail, sayin'
>
> God is a God! God don't never change!
> God is a God an' He always will be God!

These musical sermons proclaim that God does not fail nor change. They preach that God can be depended upon even though God is clearly transcendent.

> Mah God is so high, yuh can't get over Him;
> He's so low, yuh can't git under Him;
> He's so wide, yuh can't get aroun' Him;
> Yuh mus' come in by an through de Lam'.

God is high, low, and so wide, yet the singing preacher can still testify that God is "mah God" and God can "fill mah heart wid His love." God is cosmic but also personally present in "mah heart." Thus God is not far away in the biblical past or eschatological future. God is in the present tense of our day. "My Lord's a-writin' all de time . . ." God is eternally present and active in today's world. LaRue asserts that "blacks use language to render God present." In one of his own sermons supporting this point, LaRue proclaims,

> God shall reign supreme. There is not when he was not, and there cannot be when he shall not be. He's back behind yesterday and he's up in front of tomorrow. Waves from two eternities dash upon his throne and yet he remains the same. He's older than time and senior to eternity. He was before was was. Back before the purple hills of eternity, before there was a who or a where a when or the, God was.[85]

Though LaRue preaches that "God was," his point is that "God is" and will forever be. This is significant for generating hope because it proclaims that even when no one else or nothing is left, God is and will be present. In the midst of joy and sorrow, celebration and lament, God is present. This is the heart of spiritual preaching that desires to generate hope—a present God.

The presence of God is not explained per se but proclaimed. God's proximity to humanity in whatever circumstance is declared. When the black bard sings, "Why not every man?," since the Lord delivered Daniel, the singing preacher is making a claim that God is present to deliver every person. God is in the present tense and can be encountered. Traditionally, African American preaching promotes "experiential encounter."[86] The ultimate aim is not the conveying of information about God but facilitating an encounter with God, God's transforming power in the lives of the hearers. As Henry Mitchell writes, "There is a radical difference between listening to an essay designed to enlighten and listening to a Word desperately needed to sustain life."[87] In the valley of dry bones, God is desperately needed to sustain hope. Gerhard Forde writes, "A sermon does indeed include explaining, exegeting, and informing, but ultimately it must get around to and aim at a doing, an actual pronouncing, declaring, giving of the gift. . . . We must learn to speak a Word that not only explains but does something."[88] Spiritual preaching *does* hope by offering and proclaiming God. It attempts to give God to those listening. It invites God to be present for those in the pews because through encounter with God, hope arises. Hope will not be generated by preaching *about* hope. A preacher actually needs to preach hope for the possibility of generating hope. In this case, preaching a present God will help move one in that direction.

In a sermon, "Hold On to Your Hope," based on Ezekiel 37:13-14, Teresa Fry Brown merges the relationship of a present God and hope. She proclaims,

> The truth is that nothing is too hard for God
> It is not over until God says it is over
> Hopelessness became hope in Ezekiel's vision
> > Death became life
> > God's promise was affirmed
> > Reconciliation was actualized
> God understands that sometimes the mountains seem too high
> > and the valleys seem too low
> > Some of us shout on Sunday, but face Monday burdened
> > > with cares
> > Sometimes, no matter how hard we try, all hell regularly
> > > breaks loose
> > > in our lives
> God wants us to know today there is a plan to preempt the death
> > of hope.[89]

Later in this same sermon, she says, "God says Hope is not dead."[90] Brown proclaims a present God by speaking of God in the present tense. "God understands," "God wants us to know," and "God says" are ways to help the hearer comprehend the real presence of the divine in today's world. Of course, this does not guarantee God's presence but it does signify how God can be present now. By having God say, "Hope is not dead," the hearer may come to hear God's voice. Brown's aim is not to teach about God but to preach God in a manner that would generate hope in others, to encourage them to keep on keepin' on because of God's presence. This sermon offers a living God who says it is not over. This is vital because "Genuine hope comes . . . only in relationship to God."[91] To forget God is, as Don Saliers writes, "an act of worshipping false hopes—our idols."[92] Remembering and proclaiming God is in fact the reason why "the African American church is a celebration in oppression."[93] Hope due to God's presence provides good reason for people to celebrate in the midst of death.

That God is present is fundamental to spiritual preaching that hopes to generate hope in others, along with preaching the tension and a vision. These homiletical approaches to generating hope follow the lead of the spiritual homiletical tradition and work in collaboration with a hermeneutical approach to Scripture that is also grounded in the spirituals. The final chapter will explore how the spirituals can help preachers read Scripture for the purpose of preaching Christian hope.

You Shall Live

Reading the Bible for Preaching Hope (and Death)

> *. . . I will cause breath to enter you, and you shall live.*
>
> —Ezek. 37:5

> *There is a balm in Gilead.*
>
> —Traditional

The ending of chapter 1 pointed to several reasons why remembering the spirituals is important for preaching today. Remembering the spirituals, musical sermons, may actually help re-member the ministry of preaching hope. This look backward may actually aid preachers to look forward into a future that includes realistic, hope-filled proclamation. This particular cultural historical memory is interconnected with the future of homiletical hope. If one intends to preach hope, one must then read the Bible hopefully, without neglecting little deaths. The spirituals function as guides for this as well. Therefore, here I focus on the sermon preparation process, exploring how one may read Scripture for the purpose of preaching hope in light of how the spirituals handle biblical interpretation in their musical sermons.

The Bible is one of the critical resources the spirituals draw upon, as is true in any preaching, but this does not mean that the relationship of African Americans to the Bible has been without tension. However, Scripture has always played an important role in African American sermons, including the spirituals, and *how* Scripture is read or interpreted in them will be illuminating for exploring a hermeneutics of hope for contemporary preaching that occurs in the domain of death. Clearly, declaring "the Bible says" is not enough to proclaim hope to those who are dying in the valley of life. A spiritual preacher will aim for resurrection and thus declare "You shall live," but it will become evident that it takes more than reiterating the Bible to do this.

Ezekiel and Resurrection

The homiletical metaphor of the valley of dry bones reveals that death is the context of preaching, highlights the vital presence of the Spirit in preaching, and affirms the power of the spoken word through the work of the Spirit. But Ezekiel also discloses the ultimate outcome of the interaction of the Spirit and the word in the domain of death—resurrection. Preaching in the Spirit results in the restoration of hope through the resurrection of the dead. As noted already, when Ezekiel prophesies to the dry bones in chapter 37, the "breath" or "spirit" is linked to new life so Ezekiel can say, "You shall live" (vv. 5, 6, 14), or "They may live" (v. 9), or "They lived" (v. 10). This scene of resurrection is not an overnight fix, however; it happens in stages among the bones. Resurrection is not necessarily immediate (Jesus even knew this!), because when Ezekiel prophesies the "bones came together, bone to its bone . . . and there were sinews on them, and flesh had come upon them, and skin had covered them; but there was no breath in them" (vv. 7-8). There was no spirit or life in them. They were the walking dead, empty shells of flesh and skin, with no life. They were zombies and many times that is the plight of Christian congregations—not the literal dead, but the figurative dead, in need of resurrection and hope. John Levison writes, "there can . . . be the form of the body without spirit pulsing and moving within."[1]

This may be true for many churches and other institutions that are only shells of an ancient past without any present substance; preaching can be a ministry among zombies. They may look right and act right but still be dead because there is no breath, spirit, in them. They have sinews and flesh, their surface appears constructive, but below the surface is only stale death. There is no sign of life or breath in them. This may even be true for theologians and ethicists who possess theological and philosophical systems that have nothing to do with the real, down-to-earth practices of the church that will make a difference in society. This occurs because they are in fact the "slain" ones (v. 9) though they appear to be alive. Their theories and practices are thin theologically and only vestiges of a glorified colonial past of the "good ol' days." These walking-dead zombies, however, do not halt the resurrection homiletic because being dead is fertile soil into which the wind can breathe life. Death is ripe for resurrection when preachers embrace the Spirit blowing in the valley of dry bones. Though the resurrection is not immediate, it eventually occurs. It takes time, but it does happen. It may not come when you want it, but it will happen in God's time. The many dry bones were "lying in the valley" (v. 2), but because of the inspiration of the Spirit of God, the "vast multitude" eventually "stood on their feet" (v. 10). They were down, but they got up.

This is a clear visual corporeal image of resurrection in the midst of death. Spiritual preaching aims to help people get back up, to rise from death's ash heap. It is a collective or corporate resurrection because God lets Ezekiel know that "these bones are the whole house of Israel" (v. 11). They were the ones who had lost hope and were "dried up" and "cut off" (v. 11). But because of the work of the Spirit through words, "they lived" (v. 10). Even if preachers want to avoid resurrection talk, the metaphor of Ezekiel in this valley does not allow them to do so. The aim of preaching in the Spirit through this lens is clearly resurrection. It is unavoidable, with its use of the image of graves. Twice, through Ezekiel, God says, "I am going to open your graves, and bring you up from your graves, O my people" (vv. 12-13). Like a good sermon, God makes the message clear through repetition. The people were dead in graves but God will cause them to rise out of their graves. This is the ultimate end of God's story for God's people—resurrection. This visionary occurrence of resurrection ("open your graves," "bring you up from your graves") for the Jewish community points to the affirmation of the unique power and knowledge of the Lord. God stirs this revivification so that "You shall know that I am the LORD" (v. 6), a phrase repeated more than fifty times throughout the book of Ezekiel. Preachers will do well to know who is God and who does resurrection through human speech. Ezekiel's vision will not allow preachers to be fooled into thinking we are God when in fact we are just mere mortals

(vv. 3, 9, 11). "Can these bones live?" is a question that only God can answer, making Ezekiel declare, "O LORD God, you know" (v. 3).

Only God is God. This passage affirms this and Ezekiel implies that "God is a God! God don't never change! God is a God an' he always will be God!" The overarching message that the dead might live again is full of hope, not only for Israel, but for us. Preaching in the Spirit may not only restore hope to those who have lost it, but spark a resurrection of the dead. This is important especially if one believes that preaching is a "ministry of raising the dead."[2] Spiritual preaching trusts God enough to believe that resurrection is possible in the valley of dry bones but it also affirms that church pews are full of dying people in need. Not every preacher may have such a vision. Some may envision the purpose of preaching to be otherwise, perhaps along the lines of a hospice ministry where people receive help to die with dignity rather than raising them to new life in Christ. Yet preaching in the Spirit is a resurrection ministry of hope. Thus spiritual preachers preach for resurrection and the restoration of hope. In the valley, preaching begins with mortification but it ends with vivification. The word will not only be that "He 'rose" but that "You will rise" and "You shall live." The collective bodily resurrection of Israel alludes to the biblical witness of physical resurrection where the dead can be raised (1 Kgs. 17:17-24; 2 Kgs. 4:18-37; Luke 24). A physical bodily revival will only occur at the end of time, the eschaton (1 Cor. 15:12-58). This is a future hope, but even in the present people can experience a foretaste of the resurrection when they experience new life in their dry lives.

Christian preachers who take Ezekiel and resurrection to heart will realize that "The heart of the Christian faith is Easter. Jesus Christ is risen. A new age has begun. The power of death has been broken. This is both a promise of the future and the character of hope that already breaks into our present."[3] Resurrection is possible and preferable for preaching that really wants to have an impact on today's world of death. In light of Ezekiel and the hope of resurrection, there is already a theological bias when one goes to the biblical text in order to do interpretive work for preaching that will stir life. Resurrection is a theological lens, a hermeneutic of hope, for reading the Bible for preaching hope. If one believes in the resurrection by faith, one will approach Scripture through the lens of "open graves." It will take courage to face death and the grave and to declare to whatever is dead, "You shall live." With God's power, this is possible as graves will open. Thus in the valley of dry bones it is essential to have "a 'he got up' hermeneutic . . . in our homiletic."[4]

The Spirituals' Relationship to the Bible

Before delving into the spiritual hermeneutics of hope, it is important to note the historical relationship between the spirituals and the Bible. The slave religious experience included the Bible. The Bible was one of the main sources for the spirituals, to such an extent that Brian Chenu states, "The spirituals were born through the fertility of Scripture."[5] Though that may be an overstatement, one cannot deny the "deep biblicism"[6] of the spiritual homiletical tradition. There are specific biblical references and overtones throughout the spirituals like "Joshua fit de battle of Jericho" or "Ezekiel saw de wheel." One might even call the spirituals a distinct representation of so-called biblical preaching. Biblical imagery and themes pervade the spirituals, giving them a scriptural repertoire useful for effective proclamation. John Work even states "that if the Bible should be lost, it could be recovered and reconstructed from the mind of the Negro."[7] The enslaved, the unknown black-bard preachers, were immersed into the Bible through slavery and its interaction with Christianity. Thus the world of the Bible, the Old and New Testaments, permeates the singing, preaching, and story-telling of the enslaved to such an extent that some have called the spirituals the "Third Testament." This in turn suggests the importance of Scripture for preaching. There is a biblical orientation in spiritual preaching. The sacred pages of the Bible are plowed for a word from the Lord for the people. One cannot deny the spirituals' close connection to the Bible and as "a 'classic' in African American religion . . . [spirituals] can serve as guides for African American theological interpretations."[8] This includes interpretation of the Bible for the purpose of preaching today. There has been a certain reverence and respect for the Bible as a "Holy Book" throughout black history, but just because one takes the Bible seriously does not mean that one has to take it literally.

Spiritual preaching exemplified by the spirituals is neither naïve nor locked into literalistic interpretations of Scripture. This is vitally important for thinking about preaching hope because one may preach the text literally yet never preach the gospel of Jesus Christ. Spiritual preaching reveals that preaching involves more than the Bible though one still relates to the Bible for the purpose of preaching. James Cone explores this point in *The Spirituals and the Blues*:

> In regard to biblical literalism it is of course true that slaves were not biblical critics and thus were unaware of European academic reflections on the origins of biblical writings emerging in response to the

Enlightenment. Like most of their contemporaries, they accepted the inerrancy of scripture. But in contrast to white 'fundamentalists' the black preachers have never been enslaved to the *words* of scripture. The texts of the Bible served as starting points for an interpretation consistent with existence of the folk.[9]

For the old-time black preacher, "A text served mainly as a starting point and often had no relation to the development of the sermon. Nor would the old-time preacher balk at any text within the lids of the Bible."[10] For many African American preachers, the Bible has always been an important resource for preaching without the endorsement of bibliolatry. Spiritual preaching gets close to the Bible but also keeps its distance. The Bible is a starting point but not the ending point in preaching.

There is more to preaching than the biblical text. In the spiritual hom-iletical tradition, there is even musical intonation of the gospel story. In one case that James Weldon Johnson cites, when a preacher began with a dull sermon, "The congregation sat apathetic and dozing. He sensed that he was losing his audience and his opportunity. Suddenly he closed the Bible, stepped out from behind the pulpit and began to preach. He started intoning . . ."[11] Though rich in biblical imagery, the spirituals reveal that for preaching hope the Bible is not enough. In the previous example, the Bible is "closed." Preaching hope goes beyond the Bible and it may even require singing, intoning. This is why approaching the Bible literally did not have much traction unless it was for life-giving and liberating resurrec-tion reasons. Cone asserts,

> the black preacher was literal only about what he believed God would do for the people. The very literalism of black religion supported a gospel of earthly freedom. Black people were literal when they sang about Daniel in the lion's den, David and Goliath, and Samson and the Philistines. On the other hand they dispensed with biblical liter-alism when white people began to use the cure of Ham and Paul as evidence that blacks ought to accept their slavery.[12]

Literal readings of Scripture occurred for aims of liberation and freedom. Otherwise, they appear to dispense with them. Spiritual preaching believes literally the gospel of a delivering God but not the Bible—the story and not the text. Thus, though the spirituals are close to the Bible for preaching as a starting point, spiritual preachers still close the Bible when it is time to declare a word from the Lord. When it comes to reading the Bible for preaching hope (and death), it takes more than a retelling of the text. It requires knowing and telling the story of God for the people of God in the past, present, and future.

The story is important because of the way many blacks learned the Bible. In the context of slavery, the Bible was introduced as reinforcing proslavery ideology though many were skeptical of these oppressive interpretations. The Bible may be deemed "the book of slavery's children,"[13] including the unknown black bards, but what is vital when considering how one approaches the interpretation of Scripture is how the spiritual preachers are not beholden to the *text* of the book but to the *story* of the book, to the word of God and not the words of the text. Albert Raboteau concurs when he writes, "Unable to read the Bible for themselves and skeptical of their masters' interpretation of it, most slaves learned the message of the Christian Gospel and translated it into songs in terms of their own experience."[14] The gospel message appropriate for their situation was critical for them. Written words were not the main channel for the word of God, but hymns and spirituals conveyed the gospel story through "the powers of listening and memory."[15] The oral/aural teaching and learning mode of the gospel message allowed for a fluid and free interpretation of the story based on one's situation. The enslaved could not be bound to texts because during this time they were banned from learning to read the Bible. There were laws against teaching slaves to read but, despite this prohibition, they learned the gospel story that enabled them to really "read" what God was doing in their world.

The story took priority over the text, thus "the text serves the story and not the other way around."[16] This story had to do with God's continual work of freedom among the oppressed, the least and the left out. This means that the context out of which the spirituals arose always required preaching to be more than the text because texts have been used to oppress real human bodies, especially black and brown bodies. Spiritual preaching is always more than a reiteration of the Bible. It is a retelling of the liberating gospel of God and how that gospel story intersects with human experience. Though the gospel story is more important than biblical texts, the spirituals are interlocked with the Bible, as mentioned. The Bible is still important for spiritual preaching. John Lovell writes, "The Bible of the spiritual writer is not everybody's Bible and is not the Bible of the theologian or of any doctrinaire Biblical philosopher. It is a thin Bible with some names and events recurring quite often, others mentioned but rarely, and still others of alleged importance never mentioned. It is a source book, not a textbook or a book of rules."[17] Though such characters as Ruth, Esther, Solomon, Isaiah, and Jeremiah are not prominent in the spirituals, if they are even mentioned, the Bible still has high standing as a key conversation partner and source for Christian proclamation as this spiritual dictates:

> Holy Bible, Holy Bible,
> Holy Bible, book divine, book divine—
> Before I'd be a slave, I'd be buried in my grave,
> And go home to my Father and be saved.[18]

Despite the ambivalent relationship between black peoples and the Bible historically, the Bible plays an important role in the ministry of preaching, as the spirituals demonstrate. Spiritual preaching necessitates conversation with Scripture, even if one eventually closes it as did the old-time preachers. In preaching, one "must contend with the Bible."[19] A preacher wrestles with the biblical text until God pours out a blessing. "What one needs to get the preaching job done comes with some kind of encounter with Scripture."[20] Once a preacher encounters Scripture, the question becomes "What will I do with it?" and "How will I read it for preaching hope?" The spirituals, despite how the Bible may have been interpreted for destructive and deathly aims at times, appropriate, read, and handle biblical texts for life-giving purposes, for resurrection.

The Bible can be used to destroy and demonize others but the Bible in preaching can also be harnessed to build up and give hope to others. Spiritual preaching may possess a hermeneutics of suspicion toward biblical texts but there must also be a hermeneutics of trust toward Scripture if there is going to be a hermeneutics of hope on the path toward generating hope in others and resurrecting them. The imagined ends of preaching shape the means. If one hopes for hope then one should read the Bible in a hopeful manner with a hermeneutic of hope. As one engages the Bible for the task of preaching, through the lens of resurrection hope the issue becomes *how* one reads Scripture for the purpose of preaching. The spirituals as sermons utilized the Bible to give life, not death, to create hope, not hurt. This is the Spirit(ual) trajectory blowing out of the valley of death. The way the spirituals read Scripture with a hermeneutics of hope can help contemporary preachers open graves in their ecclesial cemeteries.

Spiritual Hermeneutics for Preaching

The living gospel story learned orally took precedence over biblical texts in the time of slavery, thus what is not found on the pages of the sacred pericope has priority in spiritual preaching. That is, what is heard, felt, believed, and experienced takes priority over words on a page. In fact, a *spiritual* hermeneutics of hope for the purpose of preaching hope does not start with the Bible, but it begins with human experience and need, even before it asserts a belief in a caring, liberating God and actually engages Scripture in some way. These three aspects of a *spiritual* hermeneutics of hope—attention to human need, belief in God, engagement with Scripture—will now be discussed.

Attentiveness to Human Need

Spiritual preaching begins with humanity and exegesis of the human landscape because people have priority in the spiritual homiletical tradition. As Sojourner Truth once said, "I don't read such small stuff as letters. I read men and nations."[21] Preachers read people first then texts later. In his work on cultural interpretation Brian Blount writes that, for the spiritual,

> the interpretive move is from experience to biblical image, not the other way around. The slaves' critical starting point is their historical human circumstance. The biblical images become a means of understanding and enduring the pivotal reality that is their present moment. . . . Their key intent is not so much to understand the Bible as it is to understand their historical circumstance. The Bible becomes an interpretative means rather than an interpretive end.[22]

This is why "the Bible says" is not enough for preaching hope, because a preacher should determine what the Bible says in relation to *us*, human experience. Spiritual preachers read the Bible through experience, causing some to declare that social location conditions biblical interpretation. What is important for our purposes is that "what the Bible means has priority over what the Bible meant."[23] The *sitz im leben* of the text is insufficient for preaching the gospel. It is vital to engage the Bible in light of human experience. The Bible is not just historical narrative, but somehow becomes the human story, a reflection of present humanity, thus one reads Scripture for what it reveals about human experience. Samuel Proctor writes, "The Bible . . . relates to real life situations because it comes from and draws on real life situations."[24] The accent is on "real-life situations" in spiritual preaching.

The spirituals pay attention to human experience as effective preaching does but it goes a step further to attend to human need within that experience. To proclaim hope in the domain of death, one must develop sensitivity toward human need in order to determine to whom and to what the sermon is supposed to minister. The spirituals reveal that human need is a critical lens through which one approaches Scripture for preaching hope. This implies that life is not always a bunch of sweet-smelling roses but includes thorns as well. There is great need, little deaths, all around. Preachers who want to proclaim hope need an awareness of the human situation in need of real hope. The women I mentioned in the introduction became disillusioned with Creflo Dollar's prosperity message because life is more than prosperity and indeed includes pain and suffering. One preaches hope because there is the presence of hurt in humanity. Thus knowing what the human need is in the listening audience is vital for the effective proclamation of Christian hope. One homiletician notes that most people go to Scripture because they "are lead there by their pain and their problems."[25] Real-life issues and situations are the starting point in the hermeneutical enterprise of preaching hope. Before the text, there is the human and frequently humans are in a valley of dry bones.

There are very many bones, thus the human need is communal. One is attuned to a collective human need in this valley just as Ezekiel shows a collective resurrection. Spiritual preaching "speaks to the life of an oppressed people"[26] in particular. Spiritual preachers read Scripture for the life and hope of a community, for the resurrection of the dead. The unknown origins of the spirituals imply this communal interpretive lens that pays close attention to the unknown, untaught, and unnamed. The deep needs of humanity shape how one approaches Scripture and provide the reason why one approaches the Bible in the first place. These needs are primary and shape the contour of the hope that is eventually proclaimed. A hermeneutics of hope recognizes that "Texts are read not only within contexts; a text's meaning is also dependent upon the pretext(s) of its readers."[27] If a preacher is predisposed toward the context of human need, this will lead one to wrestle with the text until one is blessed with meaningful hope to preach. Without a clear sense of the human need, it is most likely that the hope proclaimed will lack clarity as well. Thus attentiveness to human need is an essential beginning in spiritual hermeneutics for preaching. The following spiritual does not just proclaim the resurrection

of Jesus but links the hope of resurrection to one's own situation and circumstance. It becomes a personal testimony or story of how "the Lord
shall bear my spirit home."

> He 'rose, He 'rose, He 'rose from the dead
> He 'rose, He 'rose, He 'rose from the dead
> And the Lord shall bear my spirit home.

In this case, the resurrection is appropriated for one's existential reality,
for one's "spirit." Whatever is the human need, it is insufficient to just tell
the story of Jesus as found in the Bible. It is critical to see how that story
relates to the human situation and then proclaim that.

A preacher attends to human need then attends to the biblical text in
light of the human need. One interprets Scripture for preaching according
to the human need. Following the spiritual homiletical tradition means
to follow the enslaved who "took from their hearing and reading of the
Bible what was useful and left the rest."[28] Even with the priority of human
need, one must remember that the Bible was and is still respected as a
sacred book though there is hermeneutical freedom from the Bible because
human bodies are more important than Bibles. Spiritual preachers proclaim "whatever he [or she] believes necessary for the people."[29] The Bible
is a source for preaching hope but the eyes of the preacher read the Bible
with the eyes of human need. One does not interpret Scripture for Scripture's sake but reads it for the life of a people who are in great need.

> Keep a-inchin' along, keep a-inchin' along,
> Massa Jesus is comin' bye an' bye,
> Keep a-inchin' along like a po' inch worm,
> Massa Jesus is comin' bye an' bye.

This musical sermon reads the life situation through the lens of nature,
an inchworm, the Bible, and Jesus, and forges a message out of this inter-
relationship in light of the perceived need of the hearer in the moment.
This sermon sings to the community to keep on keepin' on because of the
eventual advent of Jesus. Preachers may "take a text" but the question
remains, "How do they handle it in light of human need?" Meaning in
the preaching moment arises when one is attentive to human experience
and need. As Frank Thomas argues, "Perception of meaning is limited if
traditional exegesis separates sources from existential suffering, tragedy,

and evil."[30] But existential reality does not encompass the whole hermeneutics of hope under discussion. Without attentiveness to human need,
there can be no preaching of hope, yet without a theological hermeneutic
that includes a liberating and loving God, there can also be no proclamation of hope.

Belief in a Loving, Liberating God

A second critical component of the spiritual hermeneutics for preaching is
a belief in a loving, liberating God. Note that this hermeneutical approach
has not yet reached engagement with Scripture. One begins with human
need and the reality of God. One exegetes the situation of humanity and
exegetes the work of divinity. What a preacher discovers and believes
about these two is brought to biblical interpretation. It is blatantly obvious
that spiritual preaching is theocentric because deep in the cultural recesses
of historical memory is the belief that "God cared for [the enslaved] despite
the cruel vicissitudes of life."[31] The spirituals asserted that a God who did
not care did not count. God cares so much that God is "a God who gets
to us by getting with us—Immanuel!"[32] That God is love (1 John 4:8) and
loves the world (John 3:16), including the marginalized and ostracized,
is at the heart of spiritual preaching. Gardner Taylor sums it up when he
says, "Never miss the central thrust of it all—God reaching out in this way
and that for a people whom He loves . . ."[33]

God not only loves but also has the power to liberate and set free those
who are oppressed and depressed. God is a God who can and will do something and not just sit idly by in a Starbucks sipping a caramel macchiato. A
foundational piece of this hermeneutics of hope is belief in a God who acts
mightily on behalf of the oppressed. God liberates the least of these and
continues to act in human history for justice. God is good all the time and
"in all situations, there exists a divine sense of unquestionable ability."[34]
Blount asserts it this way about the enslaved: "[They] considered their historical predicament seriously but did not believe that the evil it constituted
was a fated given that could never be overturned. Because they saw God
acting in history, they not only believed that there would be a divine, otherworldly revolution, but that God would, with human assistance, inau-
gurate revolutionary activity here on earth as well . . ."[35] Thus, despite the
troubled waters of life, the spiritual preachers could sing "God's a-gonna
trouble de water" and encourage others to "wade in the water" regardless
of the situation because God was working in the water. God was going

to trouble the trouble and bring healing and liberation. God is active and moving, pulsating in the veins of creation. As noted earlier, "There is at the heart of life a Heart."[36]

That God loves and liberates is an essential part of preaching hope and reading Scripture for preaching hope. Regardless of destructive interpretations of the Bible that aim for demonization of the other, the spirituals proclaim that God will win and ultimately defeat evil. This is possible in spiritual preaching because it does not suffer from bibliolatry and worship of the Bible. Rather, the spiritual homiletical tradition worships God and God is not confined to a written canon and is bigger than a book, *the* Book. Spiritual preaching is in service to a God who loves the least of these, the unwanted, the unknown, the unnamed, and works to liberate them despite opposition. There is a deep sense of the "gospel of God's 'somehow'" embedded in this preaching approach.[37] As Isaac Rufus Clark once taught, "Just as [the] sun never fails [to rise or set], God never fails. Morning always comes."[38] Through this belief in a loving and liberating God who never fails in relation to human need, the preacher then approaches the Bible for a word from the Lord for a people.

Engaging the Bible

In light of what has been said about attentiveness to human need and the belief in a loving, liberating God, what follows will reveal another critical piece of the spiritual hermeneutics for preaching: engaging the Bible. This section will detail particular ways that the spirituals read or handle Scripture in their sermons for the purpose of preaching hope. I do not attempt to be exhaustive but, rather, suggestive in terms of the possibilities that the spirituals offer to preachers. Despite beginning with human need and God, the Bible is eventually engaged, wrestled with, for a blessing from God for God's people in need. Spiritual preaching does not worship the Bible but converses with the Bible, partnering with it for fruitful proclamation. The spiritual homiletical tradition provides some useful reading strategies on the path toward the proclamation of hope. I will present eight strategies, in no particular order of priority, which may be useful for preachers who desire to preach hope (and death).

1. *Using the biblical text as a "mirror" of the human situation.* This may be called a *reflection reading*. When the preacher turns toward the Bible to gaze at it, he or she sees a reflection of the world in it. The human story correlates with or is analogous to the biblical story; it is not the actual

historical biblical story, but it is similar in metaphorical or figurative ways. Most prominent in the spiritual homiletical tradition is the exodus motif in such spirituals as "Go Down, Moses": "Go down, Moses, 'Way down in Egypt's land, / Tell old Pharaoh, Let my people go!" From what has already been said about this spiritual, it is clear that the exodus story is historically paradigmatic for African Americans as an archetypal myth through which one reads the Bible for liberation aims. In this antiphonal song, the chorus joins in on "Let my people go," accenting the divine liberatory call. This spiritual stresses that God is a God of liberation of the oppressed. As noted already, blacks have seen themselves as Israel, God's chosen people, who are suffering under the hand of Pharaoh, the white oppressors, in the land of Egypt, America. God calls for freedom, "Let my people go," and eventually leads the enslaved out of slavery into a promised land of hope. Thus the exodus narrative has been read as not only the story of Israel but the story of African Americans who have seen their own reflection in the biblical account.

This does not mean that every detail of the biblical text is explored in the spiritual; clearly, this is not so. The musical sermons consist of a poetic compression despite the elongation of the actual narrative. Spiritual preachers emphasize certain parts of the biblical story based on perceived need. In this case, "Let my people go" is emphasized. But in the Bible God actually tells Moses to tell Pharaoh "Let my people go, so that they may worship me" (Exod. 4:23; 7:16). The spiritual does not include this call to worship God. It is as if the enslaved were fed up with servitude and did not want even to include service to God in the song, but only the delivering actions of God on their behalf. Thus this musical sermon is not an exact or literal account of the biblical text because the text is used only as a mirror, a reflection of human life. The human need was freedom; thus that is highlighted. "Didn't ol' Pharaoh get lost, Get lost, get lost, In the Red Sea, true believer . . ." The call for liberation and the eventual liberation is what the singing preacher proclaims.

Thurman notes, "What they had found true in their experience lived for them in the sacred Book," yet the enslaved took "many liberties" with the ideas found in the Bible.[39] There were parallels with their lives in the biblical text and a particular resonance with Old Testament themes and stories. If God could lock the lion's jaw for Daniel (Dan. 6:1-28)—"Didn't my Lord deliver Daniel?"—and deliver the children of Israel out of Egypt (Exodus 14), God could deliver them from slavery. Lawrence Levine writes, "These songs state as clearly as anything the manner in which the sacred world of the slaves was able to fuse the precedents of the past, the conditions of the present, and the promise of the future in one connected reality." The past biblical stories became immediate present stories of their human reality in a future present sacred time.[40] The mirror of the biblical text is so clear that spiritual preachers can sing, "*We* are climbing Jacob's ladder," and not just Jacob, because we see ourselves in the reflection of the biblical text. Reading the Bible as a mirror of the human situation causes "the Book" to be a display of "very real accounts"[41] and "not flat accounts but apertures in the everyday world."[42] Thus hope arises from the fact that what God did then, God can still do now in relation to human need.

2. *Retelling the biblical text or theme through amplification.* In other words, this is an *amplified reading.* This is poignantly expressed in the spirituals that center on Jesus' suffering. The idea or theme of Jesus' suffering is emphasized by repetition and general amplification of the overall idea. Reiteration of an exact biblical text is not the focus but retelling the biblical theme of his passion as told through the Gospels in a rhetorically heightened manner is the goal. For instance, the refrain of "Calvary" amplifies the cross not only through repetition of that word but through a rising and falling melodic line:

> Calvary, Calvary, Calvary, Calvary,
> Calvary, Calvary, Surely He died on Calvary.

The more popular spiritual "Were You There?" uses each verse to take one deeper into the story of the suffering of Christ. Though the focus of each verse is a bit different, the basic idea is still the same and this comes through the melodic repetition, thus amplifying the pain and eventual death of Jesus. "Were you there when they crucified my Lord? . . . Were you there when they nailed Him to the tree? . . . Were you there when they pierced Him in the side? . . . Were you there when the sun refused to shine? . . . Were you there when they laid Him in the tomb?" This approach to the Bible is an attempt to get the hearer "there," in the particular pathos of pain in this case. Sometimes, a specific piece of the biblical story may be highlighted as with "He nevuh said a mumbalin' word, not a word, not a word, not a word" (John 19:9; Mark 15:3-5; Luke 23:8-9) but this, too, is repeated again and again to amplify a particular part of the story. The story in the text is what is important in this approach. This does not exempt the idea of the text as a mirror but the sense of story is heightened through amplification. The preacher wants to get the story straight and highlight that in ways that bring others into the biblical story.

The approach of amplification also occurs in relation to stories of good news. Numerous parts of Scripture talk about the kingdom of God. This biblical theme is taken up in numerous spirituals in a heightened fashion to retell the story about God's kingdom.

> Got a crown up in de Kingdom, ain't dat good news?
> Got a crown up in de Kingdom, ain't dat good news?
> I'm a goin' to lay down dis world,
> Goin' to shoulder up mah cross,
> Goin' to take it home to Jesus,
> Ain't dat good news?

This spiritual, "Ain't Dat Good News?," amplifies the good news of going to the divine kingdom by repeating the basic sentiment and changing only one word in each verse: "Got a harp . . . Got a robe . . . Got a slippers . . . Got a Savior." But it is basically a retelling of the biblical theme of the kingdom of God. The overall goal of this approach to the Bible for preaching is to focus on one major idea and expand it in different ways to make sure the hearers understand the basic story because as a preacher one should know the story and be able to tell it.

3. *Seeing Jesus in the biblical text.* This is a *christological reading.* The cultural mantra in spiritual preaching was and is "Give me Jesus." As noted in the last chapter, to generate hope in preaching, preaching Jesus is critical. To get to Jesus in a sermon, a preacher should see Jesus in the biblical text. In this perspective, the Bible is a unified text. It is a canonical approach that does not "dismember the biblical text without first remembering the biblical story."[43] In reading the Bible for preaching, one wants to search for "links"[44] between various Bible passages and between the Old and New Testaments to determine if there are connections and allusions that may illuminate the meaning of the text one is studying for a sermon. Scripture can interpret Scripture but specifically in this approach, one reads the text through the lens of Christ, looking for Jesus and seeing the christological links.

Spiritual preachers read the Bible for Jesus. An illiterate slave who was a nurse to a slave master's family was taught by one of the children to recognize the name "Jesus" in the Bible. This slave became devoted to searching for "Jesus" in the Bible even though she did not know where the name could be found. Thus she opened the book randomly and "'traveled with her finger along line after line, and page after page until she found 'Jesus.'"[45] It is not that preachers search the Bible for the name "Jesus"; rather, they look for the ways a text may tell the story of Christ implicitly. In either case, Jesus is the focus. In the following spirituals, the story of Jesus Christ is linked to stories of the Old Testament.

> Oh, Mary, don't you weep, don't you mourn
> Pharaoh's army got drowned.
> Oh, Mary, don't you weep.

In this musical sermon, the resurrection power of Jesus converges with the exodus. Christ of the resurrection is connected to the God of the exodus, revealing how the exodus signifies resurrection, thus "here the reality of death and the hope of deliverance poignantly meet."[46] Though Mary weeps (John 11:28-37), her weeping will cease because Pharaoh's army got drowned; that is, God won and defeated death through the resurrection. The preacher sees Jesus in the event of the exodus. Another example of this is in the following two spirituals:

> King Jesus rides a milk-white horse, No man can hinder him.
> The river Jordan he did cross, No man can hinder him.
>
> King of kings, Lord of lords, Jesus Christ the first and the last,
> No man works like Him.
> He pitched his tent on Canaan's ground.
> No man works like Him,
> And broke the Roman kingdom down.
> No man works like Him.

In the first spiritual, the Jesus of Revelation on a white horse (Rev. 19:11-19) crosses the Jordan, not Joshua of the Old Testament, though Joshua is the one who leads Israel across the Jordan in the Bible (Josh. 3:1—4:19). In the second, Jesus conquers Canaan, not Joshua. This approach makes Joshua a type of Christ, prefiguring the work of Jesus in the New Testament.

4. *Using biblical texts to preach the whole counsel of God.* This is an *intertextual reading.* One is not confined to a little pericope because preaching entails proclaiming the gospel, the whole story, and not just the

text. A preacher takes the Bible as a whole and uses the Bible to tell the story of God, who is not boxed into one text. Many black preachers "no matter what their text or subject, may include in a single sermon references to nearly all the characters and events in the Bible—from Genesis through Revelation."[47] In the nomenclature of African American preaching traditions, one calls "the roll," the history of God's action among God's people. James Abbington presents an example of this from "Peter on the Sea," in which the first verse is about Peter but the subsequent verses of the same song speak of other biblical characters:

> Peter, Peter on the sea, sea, sea, sea!
>> Drop your nets and follow me.
> Gabriel, Gabriel, blow your trump, trump, trump, trump!
>> Blow your trumpet loud!
> Daniel, Daniel, Daniel in the lions' lions',
>> Daniel in the lions' den.
> Who, did, who did swallow Jonah, Jonah?
>> Who did swallow Jonah whole?

Abbington calls this "con-*fusing*" the different characters and events of the Bible.[48] This fusing together of various biblical characters and stories attempts to tell the whole story of God with God's people. The Old Testament is intertwined with the New, and this also occurs in the famous "There Is a Balm in Gilead" in which one verse declares, "If you cannot preach like Peter, If you cannot pray like Paul, you can tell the love of Jesus, and say 'He died for all.'" Peter, Paul, and Jesus show up to help the singing preacher preach about the divine balm. The preacher is not limited to one character or story but uses the Bible in an intertextual manner to tell the whole counsel of God.

 5. *Muting parts of the biblical text.* This may be called a *muted reading.* As I stated earlier, the enslaved were not enslaved to the Bible but attentive to human need and "could read certain parts and ignore others. . . . By the end of the century the 'Book' had come to represent a virtual language world that they could enter and manipulate in light of their social experiences."[49] Spiritual preachers are selective in their usage of the Bible according to what is needed in a particular time and place. The classic story of Howard Thurman's grandmother fits into this paradigm. She had been a slave and only allowed Thurman to read 1 Corinthians 13 and no other letter of Paul because the white ministers on the slave plantations would always

preach from Paul, "Slaves, be obedient to your masters" (Eph. 6:5). Because of this, she told Thurman that she always told herself, "that if freedom ever came and I learned to read, I would never read that part of the Bible!"[50]

Her story is a wonderful example about how certain parts of Scripture may be ignored and not viewed as useful for hopeful living. This is true in "Go Down, Moses," as noted above, but also in the following spiritual: "O, de blind man stood on the road and cried, Cryin' O, my Lord save-a me. . . . O, de blind man stood on the road and cried." The song begins and ends with a cry. In this spiritual, based on Mark 10:46-52, the blind man does not receive his sight; in the biblical text, he does. Thurman comments on this spiritual,

> [The slaves] identified themselves completely with the blind man at every point but the most crucial one. In the song, the blind man does not receive his sight. The song opens with the cry; it goes through many nuances of yearning, but always it ends with the same cry with which it began. The explanation for this is not far to seek; for the people who sang this song had not received their 'sight.' They had longed for freedom with all their passionate endeavors, but it had not come. This brings us face to face with a primary discovery of the human spirit. Very often the pain of life is not relieved—there is the cry of great desire, but the answer does not come—only the fading echo of the one's lonely cry.[51]

Though one may think that the hope in the text is the healing of the blind man, a spiritual reading of the Bible is open enough to mute certain portions of it and to suggest that the hope may be found in the lament itself based on the particular need at any given moment. A spiritual preacher does not just read the Bible but reads the human situation. In this case, the unanswered cry is preached as necessary for the path toward hope. Though "the Bible says" one thing, it does not mean that what "the Bible says" is the only thing that can be said. Saying more than the Bible takes courage in certain ecclesial settings and it takes "imaginative insight."[52]

6. *Engaging a biblical text with imaginative embellishment.* This is an *imaginative reading.* Some have called this approach "imaginative elaboration."[53] This is not repeating the text or a paraphrase of it; rather, it is what Barbara Holmes calls "African diasporan midrash," a "way of interrogating the silences and omissions of the text."[54] A classic case about heaven is when the spiritual preacher declares, "I got a robe, you got a

robe, all o'God's chillun got a robe . . . I got-a wings, you got-a wings . . . I got a harp, you got a harp, all o'God's chillun got a harp, when I get to heab'n I'm goin' to take up my harp, I'm goin' play all ovah God's Heab'n, Heab'n, Heab'n, everybody talkin' 'bout heab'n ain't goin' dere." The biblical texts about heaven do not talk about people having wings or playing harps but the spiritual brings to life creatively what heaven may be for the hearers. The Bible can function as a window into an imaginative world of hope though ultimately, preaching is more than the text.

Another spiritual, "Sister Mary Had-a but One Child," speaks of Jesus crying as a baby despite the Bible never telling of this happening, though one can rightfully assume that this was the case: "And-a every time-a that baby cried, she'd-a rock him in a weary land." Spiritual preaching goes beyond the text to an imaginative exploration of what is not said and attempts to say it in a way that relates to the people. Abbington writes, "There is probably no other vocal repertoire in the western world with such imagination and creativity in bringing the Scriptures to life like the Negro spiritual."[55] In this same imaginative mode, Teresa Fry Brown offers a sermon based on Ezekiel and the valley of dry bones and proclaims,

> "By my Spirit
> I will open up your graves
> Put the obituary aside
> Cancel the funeral arrangements . . .
> I will open up your
> Crypts of 'I can't'
> Shrines of 'I'm not smart enough'
> Mausoleums of 'It's not my fault'
> Sepulchers of 'They won't believe me'
> Resting places of 'I'm too old, too short, too poor, too dumb'
> Tombs of 'But I'm a woman. But I'm black'
> Coffins of shoulda, coulda, woulda
> Caskets of 'My family doesn't want me to be a minister'
> Sarcophagi of 'The congregation won't support me'
> Graves of 'The professor doesn't like me'"[56]

Brown takes the image of death in this text (dry bones, graves) and embellishes upon them and extends the metaphor to make it more relatable to contemporary human needs. But this is a wonderful sermonic example of how a preacher may preach with a vivid imagination that is not limited to the Bible because "the preacher cannot be content simply to tell the people what the text says."[57]

7. *Talking back to the biblical text.* This is a *responsive reading.* This strategy does not allow the Bible to have the final say but the preacher asserts his or her theological agency as a messenger of hope. The Bible may raise a question but the spiritual preacher provides the answer because of the discerned need of the hearers. In the book of Jeremiah, the prophet is joyless, grieving, and heartsick as he anticipates the imminent destruction of the people. He mournfully asks, "Is there no balm in Gilead? Is there no physician there?" (Jer. 8:18-22) A preacher could preach lament in light of this text but as noted before, historically the text has only been a starting point for black preachers. The unknown black bards approach this text by responding to it, talking back to it in light of the human situation. They sing, "There is a balm in Gilead to make the wounded whole / There is a balm in Gilead to heal the sin-sick soul." The Bible poses the question but the preacher answers it for hope to be experienced. The Bible may not say the word of hope but the gospel requires it to be spoken. The enslaved "straightened the question mark in Jeremiah's sentence into an exclamation point: 'There *is* a balm in Gilead!' Here is a note of creative triumph."[58] In this case, as in many, "the Bible says" is insufficient. Sometimes the preacher has to talk back to the Bible to get to hope.

8. *Using the biblical text to call for action in the world.* This may be called a *missional reading.* The text is a starting point for a preacher's ultimate goal. Jesus says, "You are the light of the world . . . let your light shine before others . . ." (Matt. 5:14, 16), and the spirituals take up this biblical image of "light" to call people to action in the world. Two prime examples are the following:

> Hold up yo' light you heav'n boun' solider
> Hold up yo' light you heav'n boun' solider
> Hold up yo' light you heav'n boun' solider
> Let yo' light shine aroun' de world.

> This little light of mine, I'm goin' to let it shine.
> This little light of mine, I'm goin' to let it shine.
> This little light of mine, I'm goin' to let it shine.
> Let it shine, let it shine, let it shine.

The spiritual preacher calls people to action, to shine their light and hold it up. The Bible can be a bridge or springboard to mission in the world. The text is not explained or biblical information provided but a specific point (or, in this case, image) in the text is utilized for purposes beyond the text. This keeps the preacher free from the Bible though still connected to it. The Bible is not discarded but regarded as a source for life in society. It is not so much about the biblical world as the current world, thus the image of "light" is the textual hermeneutical bridge that allows the hearers to become a part of the ongoing story of God. "Light" is not just about *that* world but this world.

These eight approaches to reading the Bible for the purpose of preaching hope as shown in the spirituals, musical sermons, are not exhaustive but should reveal that to proclaim "You shall live" requires more than quoting Scripture verses. The text, the Bible, is not enough. "The Bible says" may be an initial step but it cannot be the final step toward preaching hope in the valley of death. In fact, a spiritual preacher does not even begin with the Bible in the hermeneutical process but starts with attention to the human need of very many dry bones and a sure belief in a loving and liberating God. *Then* the spiritual preacher turns to Scripture as a conversation partner, as a source for preaching in light of the contextual, existential, and theological realities. The Bible is used, not abused. It is engaged, read, interpreted, for hopeful reasons, for resurrection aims. "You shall live" is a word in the face of death, in the midst of death. Preachers proclaim this because they not only know that humans need life but also know the God who gives it. For graves to open, it must be God who speaks through preaching because the Bible by itself cannot do it.

Imaginative Spiritual Exegesis

The previous approaches to reading the Bible for the purpose of preaching hope suggest that one comes to Scripture with a lively imagination that is bigger than the Book and enables one to see the unseen because "hope that is seen is not hope" (Rom. 8:24). Spiritual preachers engage Scripture in the ways named above as an avenue not to imprisoning one's homiletical and hermeneutical imagination within a text but freeing it to see and hear the gospel message unleashed in the world. Because human need and God take priority in a spiritual hermeneutical perspective, what one imagines the human need and nature of God to be will shape the interpretation of Scripture for preaching hope. Vincent Wimbush writes that the slave's hermeneutic [was] characterized by a looseness, even playfulness, vis-à-vis the biblical texts themselves. The interpretation was not controlled by the literal words of the texts, but by social experience. The texts were heard more than read; they were engaged as stories that seized and freed the imagination. Interpretation was therefore controlled by the freeing of the collective consciousness and imagination of the African slaves as they heard the biblical stories and retold them to reflect their actual social situation, as well as their visions for something different.[59]

What the enslaved envisioned, hoped for, had an impact on their use of the Bible for the purpose of preaching. What preachers imagine the purpose of preaching to be will shape the entire process of preaching from preparation to delivery. What one sees, imagines, affects what one says and how one says it. The valley of dry bones helps us to begin to reimagine the nature and purpose of preaching. If one never sees dry bones, one may never talk about death as the context of preaching. If one never sees open graves, one may never preach resurrection. Ezekiel 37 is a vision, thus Ezekiel imagines this scene. It is real because preaching is *really* a matter of life and death. He sees the spirit of life in the shadow of death. In fact, the Spirit is linked with his imagination, his vision (Ezek. 37:1; 3:12). This same connection is made with John in Revelation, who has visions when he is "in the spirit on the Lord's day" (Rev. 1:10).

Seeing, imagining, envisioning, is a work of the Spirit who helps preachers see and imagine what otherwise one would not be able to see. Thurman calls the human imagination a gift and writes, "The witness of God's spirit in man's spirit is symbolized by imagination, without which there could be no sense of sin, no repentance and contrition, no tenderness and sympathy, no love and no hope."[60] Imagination is not only tethered with the Spirit but vital to a hermeneutics of hope. "The problem of hopeless sermons is not the Bible; it is the familiar ways of reading it, the tools one brings to it, not seeing what is there."[61] The spirituals may challenge preachers to ask different questions of the biblical text in preparation for preaching because, as discussed, they are not only concerned with the Bible but humanity and God. One may not "see what is there" in the text because one does not ask certain questions or have particular concerns.

When approaching the Bible to do exegesis for preaching, the questions one asks of the biblical text shape the answers one receives. If one never asks about death, one may never see it. If one never asks about hope, one may never find it in order to proclaim it. If one never asks about God, God may never be preached. Thus the hermeneutical imagination is vital in moving the homiletical imagination in the direction of hope. Imagination "should permeate the whole of the exegetical exercise."[62] In the following, I will conclude this chapter by presenting particular questions that spiritual preachers may use when doing exegesis for preaching. This is not an attempt to present a full-blown exegetical method for preaching nor is it an attempt to negate traditional historical and literary critical approaches to biblical interpretation. Those and other modes of biblical criticisms are still helpful, but this is a way to tease out the specific directions the spirituals point for thinking about other ways preachers can approach biblical texts for the purpose of preaching hope. In other words, on the way to sermon development and in light of the spirituals' hermeneutical approach to reading the Bible and the history and theology of the spirituals, what types of questions should preachers ask of biblical texts if one desires to preach Christian hope? What questions will help one see *spiritually*?

Exegesis Questions

- What is the perceived human need in the context?
- What is the human need reflected in the text?
- What are the "little deaths" in the context?
- What are the "little deaths" in the text?
- What needs resurrection in the context?
- What needs resurrection in the text?
- Is there any tension in the text?
- What questions are asked of the text by the human need in the context?
- How does the text reflect the world's need, the needs of my congregation/community, or the needs of my life?
- Where do the text and context intersect?
- What does the text say about God? What is God doing?
- What is the hope expressed in the text?
- What is the relationship between God and the hope in the text?
- Do you see Jesus Christ in this passage? If so, where? What can be said about Jesus?
- Does the text have anything to do with the end, the eschaton, heaven?
- Does the text connect with any other biblical texts? How are they related?

- Is there something you want to amplify in the story (an image or idea)?
- What do you hear in the text? What are the noises or sounds in the passage?[63]
- Who or what is silent?
- What do you see in the text? Who sees and who does not see in the text?
- What are the textures in the text? What can you feel?
- What can be tasted in the text?
- What do you smell in the text?
- How does the text sound musically?
- How might you sing the text?
- What other kinds of sounds does the text cause you to make?
- What sounds may represent the text?
- What spiritual comes to mind as you read the text? What is the Spirit(ual) saying?
- What is the "mood" of the text?
- What emotions do you have as you read the text?
- Is there anything you want to mute, ignore, or resist in the text?
- Is there anything in the text that may be harmful to a human being?
- Is there something in the text that obstructs preaching hope?
- Is there anything in the text that does not connect with the situation of your community?
- Do you need to talk back to the text in any way? Why?
- Does the text raise questions that need to be answered?
- Does this text call me to action in the world? What does it call me to do?
- What does the text call me to resist, if anything?

(Open) Graves

The Hope of Preaching's Future

I am going to open your graves,
and bring you up from your graves . . .

—EZEK. 37:12

De angel roll de stone away.

—TRADITIONAL

his book has been a homiletical pilgrimage to death as an avenue
for proclaiming Christian hope. It is a response to contemporary
preaching approaches, such as prosperity-gospel preaching, that
deny the critical role of death in preaching hope and appear to erase death
from the pages of the Christian gospel; these sermons are sweet like candy
at first yet eventually sour for the soul. I took this pilgrimage with the
African American spirituals as my primary conversation partner because
these musical sermons know death, hope, and the Spirit firsthand. They
were created in a valley of dry bones, slavery's death, and if any preaching
tradition could help us think through the interplay of preaching, death,

and hope, the spiritual homiletical tradition would best do so. Thus this book excavated the landscape of the spirituals for the building of homiletical terrain. It has been a study of the spirituals for homiletical purposes, particularly as a resource for the theory and practice of preaching Christian hope today.

This journey began by establishing death as the context of preaching through a historical exploration of the setting of the spirituals that pointed to the weighty, life and death nature of preaching. The pilgrimage continued by affirming the Spirit's relationship to the spirituals and acknowledging how the Spirit speaks death and hope together through them as a way of revealing the integral connection between death and hope in preaching; lyrical analysis was important at this juncture. The journey then explored further how one might generate hope in sermons, particularly in light of the spirituals' theological stress on the eschaton and Jesus. The last leg of the journey led to how spiritual preachers might read the Bible for the purpose of preaching hope based on how the spirituals engage biblical texts. On this *spiritual* pilgrimage through this book's historical, lyrical, theological, and hermeneutical chapters, it became clear that preaching hope is inadequate without taking death seriously. Death, little deaths, should not be denied if homiletical hope is the goal for hope grows out of the dust of death. This is true for past, present, and future preaching whose ministry is in a valley of dry bones to breathe life back into the dead and dying.

The "untaught" black bards teach homiletical wisdom to help us reimagine the nature and purpose of preaching. These lessons are timely, as natural disasters, war, and disease continue to kill. Discontentment with social, political, and economic oppression continues to grow as revealed through the Arab Spring and the Occupy movement. People have died and people are dying because they want to live. They are saying like the spirituals, "No mo'," enough is enough. These are serious times for the world. Slick and sleek Spiritless prosperity saviors will not do. Only the Spirit, who leads preachers like Ezekiel to the place of death to breathe life and hope through words, can handle this situation. Courageous Spirit(ual) preachers are needed to face death because if one is not ready to die, one is not ready to preach since preaching is a matter of life and death. If one is not ready to face death, the grave, one cannot preach life and hope in any meaningful way. Preachers enter the domain of death to destroy it so that hope can rise in the world or at least in the pew. One has to face graves in order to open them by God's power. This suggests that Christian hope is not hope without death because Hope rises out of an open grave. Thus to preach Christian hope means to proclaim death, even the death of Death.

But will we risk death for resurrection and open graves? Or are we purely satisfied with dying discourses and dead sermons? Do we attempt to do ministry without Breath? Or do we collaborate with the resurrection ministry of the Spirit? If not, death will destroy us for that is preaching's context and we will just become religious sinews, flesh, and skin, without any depth or breath. Ezekiel did not need the newest Facebook fad but he surely needed the Spirit to create life out of death through his preaching. This is nothing less than the resurrection of a crucified people. In other words, every time we step into the pulpit in a valley of dry bones we proclaim the death of Death.

I began this book at a cemetery, and I will end it at another one. I write this conclusion in the season of Advent, which is also a season that reminds me of the death of my ten-year-old niece, Christiana, at whose graveside service I officiated on December 20, 2005. She suffered and died from a disease with a long name that shortened her life—juvenile dermatomyositis. For months, intravenous needles were her nails and a hospital bed her cross. Eventually her sickness stole her life. At the graveside, as her casket was lowered into the ground, seemingly Death said the benediction, the last word. But in the silence and lament of tears, there was a tiny sprout of hope that death did not have the final word and victory. My brother Dwight, the father of Christiana, his baby girl, stood up spontaneously with his family to go and look over the open grave. As they looked at the open grave and stared Death in its face, Dwight began singing Christiana's favorite worship song, "Here I am to worship, here I am to bow down . . ." What would make a father who had just lost his youngest child to death sing a song of worship?!

As he sang over death, the Spirit of life pronounced the benediction. Before dirt could be placed on top to close the grave, a divine melody slipped into the open grave in order to remind Death of its death. Hope is a song! Death did not have the final word, will not have the final say, will not win. God will win. "Thus says the Lord God: I am going to open your graves, and bring you up from your graves." In other words, "Where, O death, is your victory? Where, O death, is your sting?" (1 Cor. 15:55). The valley of dry bones is a preach-off with Death, but resurrection life will steal Death's sting and open graves. A grave, an open one, is the hope of preaching's future because it says that the future is not closed, but open for those who face it with faith and hope in God. An open grave reveals a God who got up early Sunday mornin' to defeat death. The hope of preaching is death, the death of Death.

Spiritual preaching proclaims that (little) death(s) will die. "Death will be no more; mourning and crying and pain will be no more" (Rev. 21:4). God's love is stronger than any death. Thus, whenever a preacher enters the pulpit, he or she is preaching Death's funeral. In other words, the next time you proclaim the glorious gory gospel, just tell death to "go to hell"!

Notes

INTRODUCTION. In the Middle of a Valley: The Need of Preaching

1. John Witvliet, *Worship Seeking Understanding: Windows into Christian Practice* (Grand Rapids: Baker Academic, 2003), 307.

2. Jonathan L. Walton, *Watch This! The Ethics and Aesthetics of Black Televangelism* (New York: New York University Press, 2009), 207.

3. Marvin A. McMickle, *Where Have All the Prophets Gone? Reclaiming Prophetic Preaching in America* (Cleveland: Pilgrim, 2006), 104.

4. Ibid., 116.

5. Robert M. Franklin, *Crisis in the Village: Restoring Hope in African American Communities* (Minneapolis: Fortress Press, 2007), 116. For more of Franklin's critique of the prosperity movement, see 112–26.

6. Gordon W. Lathrop, *The Pastor: A Spirituality* (Minneapolis: Fortress Press, 2006), 125. For my own critique of the overemphasis on celebration in preaching at the expense of lament, see *Spirit Speech: Lament and Celebration in Preaching* (Nashville: Abingdon, 2009).

7. Tom Long names three kinds of death in Christianity: small-*d* death, capital-*D* Death, and death in Christ. The first is natural death. The second is a "mythic force, as the enemy of all that God wills for life." The third is death in Christ as already noted. Long's use of capital-*D* Death resonates with what I call "little deaths" in this book because it is destructive in different ways whether individually, communally, or socially. His small-*d* death is what I refer to as our last death or "big" death. See Thomas G. Long, *Accompany Them with Singing: The Christian Funeral* (Louisville: Westminster John Knox, 2009), 38–41.

8. Stephanie Y. Mitchem, *Name It and Claim It? Prosperity Preaching in the Black Church* (Cleveland: Pilgrim, 2007), 122.

9. Melissa V. Harris-Lacewell, "Righteous Politics: The Role of the Black Church in Contemporary Politics," *Cross Currents* (Summer 2007): 187. For a helpful nuanced presentation of the variety within the so-called prosperity movement, see Walton, *Watch This!*

10. Milmon F. Harrison, *Righteous Riches: The Word of Faith Movement in Contemporary African American Religion* (New York: Oxford University Press, 2005), 8–12.

11. Ibid., 156.

12. Mitchem, *Name It and Claim It?* 33, 49.

13. Pastor Joel Osteen wrote a popular book with this title, *Your Best Life Now: Seven Steps to Living at Your Full Potential* (Nashville: FaithWords, 2004).

14. Walton, *Watch This!*, xiii.

15. Ibid., 201.

16. Interview with Gardner Taylor, *Religion and Ethics Newsweekly*, July 24, 2006, http://www.pbs.org/wnet/religionandethics/episodes/august-18-2006/reverend-gardner-c-taylor-extended-interview/1881/.

17. Shayne Lee, "Prosperity Theology: T. D. Jakes and the Gospel of the Almighty Dollar," *Cross Currents* (Summer 2007): 228.

18. Charles L. Campbell, *The Word Before the Powers: An Ethic of Preaching* (Louisville: Westminster John Knox, 2002), 31.

19. Lee, "Prosperity Theology," 230.

20. Marla Frederick, "'But, It's Bible': African American Women and Television Preachers," in *Women and Religion in the African Diaspora: Knowledge, Power, and Performance*, ed. R. Marie Griffith and Barbara Diane Savage (Baltimore: Johns Hopkins University Press, 2006), 285.

21. Ibid., 286.

22. James W. Perkinson, "Rap as Wrap and Rapture: North American Popular Culture and the Denial of Death," in *Noise and Spirit: The Religious and Spiritual Sensibilities of Rap Music*, ed. Anthony B. Pinn (New York: New York University Press, 2003), 134.

23. Thomas G. Long, "Chronicle of a Death We Can't Accept," *New York Times*, November 1, 2009, WK10, http://www.nytimes.com/2009/11/01/opinion/01long.html.

24. See Henry H. Mitchell, *Black Preaching: The Recovery of a Powerful Art* (Nashville: Abingdon, 1990); and Paul Scott Wilson, *The Four Pages of a Sermon: A Guide to Biblical Preaching* (Nashville: Abingdon, 1999).

25. McMickle, *Where Have All the Prophets Gone?* 89.

26. Franklin, *Crisis in the Village*, 10.

27. Perkinson, "Rap as Wrap and Rapture," 134.

28. Witvliet, *Worship Seeking Understanding*, 291. For his insights into the connections between death and weekly and annual liturgical practices, see 296–300.

29. Howard Thurman, *Deep River and The Negro Spiritual Speaks of Life and Death* (Richmond, IN: Friends United, 1975), 18.

30. John S. McClure, *Preaching Words: 144 Key Terms in Homiletics* (Louisville: Westminster John Knox, 2007).

31. Jana Childers, ed., *Purposes of Preaching* (St. Louis: Chalice, 2004).

32. For two recent works in this vein, see Long's work on funerals, *Accompany Them with Singing*, and Sally Brown's study of Christology in preaching, *Cross Talk: Preaching Redemption Here and Now* (Louisville: Westminster John Knox, 2008).

33. James Forbes, *The Holy Spirit and Preaching* (Nashville: Abingdon, 1989), 100.

34. Richard Lischer, *A Theology of Preaching: The Dynamics of the Gospel*, rev. ed. (Eugene: Wipf and Stock, 2001), 29.

35. James Earl Massey, *The Burdensome Joy of Preaching* (Nashville: Abingdon, 1998).

36. Gardner Taylor, *How Shall They Preach* (Elgin, IL: Progressive Baptist Pub. House, 1977), 24.

37. Ibid., 77–94.

38. Witvliet, *Worship Seeking Understanding*, 291.

39. Kirk Byron Jones, *The Jazz of Preaching: How to Preach with Great Freedom and Joy* (Nashville: Abingdon, 2004), 21.

40. See my book *Spirit Speech*.

41. Frederick Buechner, *Telling the Truth: The Gospel as Tragedy, Comedy, and Fairy Tale* (San Francisco: HarperSanFrancisco, 1977), 7.

42. John Blassingame, ed., *Slave Testimony: Two Centuries of Letters, Speeches, Interviews, and Autobiographies* (Baton Rouge: Louisiana State University Press, 1977), 668.

43. Mitchem, *Name It and Claim It?* 122.

44. Thurman, *Deep River*, 18.

45. Perkinson, "Rap as Wrap and Rapture," 133.

46. Toni Morrison, *Song of Solomon* (New York: Plume, 1987), 70.

47. Thurman, *Deep River*, 19.

48. John Lovell Jr., *Black Song: The Forge and the Flame* (New York: Macmillian, 1972), 112.

49. Thurman, *Deep River*, 12.

50. Lovell, *Black Song*, 198.

51. W. E. B. Du Bois, *The Souls of Black Folk* (New York: Penguin, 1969 [1903]), 265.

52. James Earl Massey, "Faith and Christian Life in the African-American Spirituals," in *God the Holy Trinity: Reflections on Christian Faith and Practice*, ed. Timothy George (Grand Rapids: Baker Academic, 2006), 57.

53. For the contour of these debates, see the works of Lovell, *Black Song*; John Work, *Folk Song of the American Negro* (New York: Negro Universities Press, 1969 [1915]); and Lawrence W. Levine, *Black Culture and Black Consciousness: Afro-American Folk Thought from Slavery to Freedom* (New York: Oxford University Press, 1977).

54. For a brief history about the popularization of the spirituals, see James Weldon Johnson and J. Rosamond Johnson, *The Books of American Negro Spirituals* (New York: Da Capo, 1969 [orig. 2 vols., 1925, 1926]), 46–50.

55. Zora Neale Hurston, *The Sanctified Church* (Berkeley: Turtle Island, 1983), 80.

56. Hurston refers to the concert-hall performances of the spirituals as the "neo-spirituals." She argues that there never has been a "genuine" spiritual presented to any audience; ibid.

57. See his poem, "O Black and Unknown Bards," in Johnson and Johnson, *Books of American Negro Spirituals*, 11–12.

58. Henry Louis Gates Jr., "Introduction: Narration and Cultural Memory in the African-American Tradition," in *Talk That Talk: An Anthology of African-American Storytelling*, ed. Linda Goss and Marian E. Barnes (New York: Simon & Schuster, 1989), 18. Please note that because my use of Ezekiel 37 is metaphoric and not the primary focus of this book, there is not a literature review nor a full-blown exegetical study of Ezekiel 37. For further study of Ezekiel in biblical scholarship, see the bibliography prepared by Jacqueline Lapsley at http://oxfordbibliographiesonline.com/obo/page/biblical-studies.

59. Allen Dwight Callahan, *The Talking Book: African Americans and the Bible* (New Haven: Yale University Press, 2006), 61.

60. James Weldon Johnson, *God's Trombones: Seven Negro Sermons in Verse* (New York: Viking Penguin, 1927), 1.

61. Two such preachers are Rubin Lacy and Carl Anderson. Rubin Lacy's sermon "Dry Bones in the Valley" is printed in Bruce Rosenberg, *Can These Bones Live? The Art of the American Folk Preacher*, rev. ed. (Urbana: University of Illinois Press, 1988),

270–79. For Carl Anderson's sermon in this tradition, see "Ezekiel and the Vision of Dry Bones," in Goss and Barnes, eds., *Talk That Talk*, 199–205.

62. Callahan, *Talking Book*, 72.

63. See Sandra L. Richards, "Dry Bones: Spiritual Apprehension in August Wilson's *Joe Turner's Come and Gone*," in *African Americans and the Bible: Sacred Texts and Social Textures*, ed. Vincent Wimbush (New York: Continuum, 2003), 743–53.

64. Dexter E. Callender, "Ezekiel," in *The Africana Bible: Reading Israel's Scriptures from Africa and the African Diaspora*, ed. Hugh R. Page Jr., et al. (Minneapolis: Fortress Press, 2010), 158.

65. Callahan, *Talking Book*, 82. For theme of exile, see also Cheryl Sanders, *Saints in Exile: The Holiness-Pentecostal Experience in African American Religion and Culture* (New York: Oxford University Press, 1999).

66. Callahan, *Talking Book*, 81, 82.

67. Ibid., 80.

68. Elsewhere, I have critiqued the overemphasis on the Bible in homiletical discourse at the expense of other critical components of preaching, namely the human body. For this perspective, see Luke Powery and Emerson Powery, "Preaching *from* Mark: Closing the Bible, Voicing the Body," in *African American Voices: Jesus and the Gospels*, ed. Thomas Slater (Atlanta: Edwin Mellen, forthcoming).

69. Witvliet, *Worship Seeking Understanding*, 300.

1. Dry Bones: Death as the Context of Preaching

1. Valentino Lassiter also calls the spirituals "musical sermons." See his *Martin Luther King in the African American Preaching Tradition* (Cleveland: Pilgrim Press, 2001).

2. Allen Dwight Callahan, *The Talking Book: African Americans and the Bible* (New Haven: Yale University Press, 2006), 77.

3. John Levison, *Filled with the Spirit* (Grand Rapids: Eerdmans, 2009), 88.

4. Allen Dwight Callahan, "Perspectives for a Study of African American Religion from the Valley of Dry Bones," *Nova Religio: The Journal of Alternative and Emergent Religions* 7, no. 1 (2003): 52.

5. Thomas G. Long, "Funeral," in *The New Interpreter's Handbook of Preaching*, ed. Paul Scott Wilson et al. (Nashville: Abingdon, 2008), 386.

6. Callahan, *Talking Book*, 76.

7. Ibid., 61.

8. Jon Michael Spencer, *Sacred Symphony: The Chanted Sermon of the Black Preacher* (New York: Greenwood, 1987), xiii.

9. Eileen Southern, *The Music of Black Americans: A History*, 2nd ed. (New York: Norton, 1983), 176.

10. C. Eric Lincoln and Lawrence Mamiya, *The Black Church in the African American Experience* (Durham: Duke University Press, 1990), 348–49.

11. John Lovell Jr., *Black Song: The Forge and the Flame* (New York: Macmillan, 1972), 166. Cf. Lincoln and Mamiya, *Black Church*, 349–50.

12. James Weldon Johnson and J. Rosamond Johnson, *The Books of American Negro Spirituals* (New York: Da Capo, 1977 [1969; orig. 2 vols., 1925, 1926]), 21–23.

13. James Weldon Johnson, *God's Trombones: Seven Negro Sermons in Verse* (New York: Viking Penguin, 1927), 10.

14. Ibid. A Mississippi ex-slave notes how slaves hummed, prayed, and sang producing a contrapuntal accompaniment to the sermon. He says, "Dey would hum deep and low in long mournful tones swayin' to an' fro. Uders would pray and sing soft while de Broder Preacher wuz a deliverin' de humble message." See Spencer, *Sacred Symphony,* 100.

15. John W. Work, *Folk Song of the American Negro* (New York: Negro Universities Press, 1969 [1915]), 83.

16. Quoted in J. Jefferson Cleveland and William B. McClain, "A Historical Account of the Negro Spiritual," *Songs of Zion* (Nashville: Abingdon, 1981), 73.

17. Work, *Folk Song,* 117.

18. Southern, *Music of Black Americans,* 176.

19. Lovell, *Black Song,* 377.

20. Work, *Folk Song,* 112.

21. Henry H. Mitchell, *Black Preaching: The Recovery of a Powerful Art* (Nashville: Abingdon, 1990), 31.

22. Work, *Folk Song,* 37.

23. Bruce Rosenberg, *Can These Bones Live? The Art of the American Folk Preacher* (Urbana: University of Illinois Press, 1988), 46, 23.

24. Ibid., 11.

25. Andrew P. Watson, "Negro Primitive Religious Services," in *God Struck Me Dead: Religious Conversion Experiences and Autobiographies of Ex-slaves,* ed. Clifton H. Johnson (Philadelphia: Pilgrim, 1969), 5.

26. Work, *Folk Song,* 37.

27. Mitchell, *Black Preaching,* 27.

28. William Turner, "Foreword," in Jon Michael Spencer, *Sacred Symphony,* ix.

29. Rosenberg, *Can These Bones Live?* 22. Unlike Rosenberg, William Turner asserts that the chanted sermon is "a source of the Black American folk song," not vice versa; see ibid., x.

30. Eugene D. Genovese, *Roll, Jordan, Roll: The World the Slaves Made* (New York: Pantheon, 1972), 266. Cf. Evans Crawford, *The Hum: Call and Response in African American Preaching* (Nashville: Abingdon, 1995). Jon Michael Spencer names seven performance parallels: melody, rhythm, call and response, harmony (e.g., use of organ), counterpoint, form, improvisation. See Spencer, *Sacred Symphony,* 100.

31. Lassiter, *Martin Luther King,* 22.

32. William Pipes, *Say Amen Brother! Old-Time Negro Preaching: A Study in American Frustration* (Detroit: Wayne State University Press, 1992 [1951]), 72. The description of the folk preacher's voice as a trombone is found in Johnson's *God's Trombones,* 7.

33. See Cheryl Townsend Gilkes, "Shirley Caesar and the Souls of Black Folk: Gospel Music as Cultural Narrative and Critique," *The African American Pulpit* 6, no. 2 (Spring 2003): 12–16.

34. William C. Turner, "The Musicality of Black Preaching: Performing the Word," in *Performance in Preaching: Bringing the Sermon to Life,* ed. Jana Childers and Clayton Schmit (Grand Rapids: Baker Academic, 2008), 205.

35. Turner, "Foreword," in *Sacred Symphony,* xi. Others who affirm the musicality of preaching in their work include Evans Crawford, Teresa Fry Brown, and Gerald Davis.

36. Kirk Byron Jones, *The Jazz of Preaching: How to Preach with Great Freedom and Joy* (Nashville: Abingdon, 2004), 30.

37. Ibid., 30.

38. Lovell, *Black Song*, 201.

39. Henry Louis Gates Jr., "Introduction: Narration and Cultural Memory in the African-American Tradition," in *Talk That Talk: An Anthology of African-American Storytelling*, ed. Linda Goss and Marian E. Barnes (New York: Simon & Schuster, 1989), 17.

40. W. E. B. Du Bois, *The Souls of Black Folk* (New York: Penguin, 1969 [1903]), 275.

41. Cheryl Kirk-Duggan, *Exorcizing Evil: A Womanist Perspective on the Spirituals* (Maryknoll, NY: Orbis, 1997), 59.

42. Johnson, *God's Trombones*, 3.

43. Lassiter, *Martin Luther King*, 9.

44. Stephen Farris, *Preaching That Matters: The Bible and Our Lives* (Louisville: Westminster John Knox, 1998), 72–74.

45. Howard Thurman, *Deep River and The Negro Spiritual Speaks of Life and Death* (Richmond, IN: Friends United, 1975), 12.

46. Albert Raboteau, *Fire in the Bones: Reflections on African-American Religious History* (Boston: Beacon, 1995), 143.

47. Thomas H. Troeger, *Wonder Reborn: Creating Sermons on Hymns, Music, and Poetry* (New York: Oxford University Press, 2010), 32.

48. Johnson and Johnson, *Books of American Negro Spirituals*, 40.

49. Farris, *Preaching That Matters*, 30–33.

50. Genovese, *Roll, Jordan, Roll*, 250.

51. Thurman, *Deep River*, 14.

52. Work, *Folk Song*, 112.

53. Mitchell, *Black Preaching*, 76–87.

54. Work, *Folk Song*, 123.

55. Thomas G. Long, *The Witness of Preaching* (Louisville: Westminster John Knox, 1989), 12.

56. Dale P. Andrews, *Practical Theology for Black Churches: Bridging Black Theology and African American Folk Religion* (Louisville: Westminster John Knox, 2002), 23.

57. Crawford, *The Hum*, 15.

58. Johnson and Johnson, *Books of American Negro Spirituals*, 11–12.

59. Work, *Folk Song*, 199; cf. ibid., 21–22.

60. Johnson and Johnson, *Books of American Negro Spirituals*, 21; cf. Zora Neale Hurston, *The Sanctified Church* (Berkeley: Turtle Island, 1983), 80.

61. Lovell, *Black Song*, 9, 13.

62. Ibid., 37.

63. Nora Tubbs Tisdale, *Preaching as Local Theology and Folk Art*, Fortress Resources for Preaching (Minneapolis: Fortress Press, 1997), 124–25; Spencer, *Sacred Symphony*, xiv; Crawford, *The Hum*, 83.

64. James Cone, *The Spirituals and the Blues: An Interpretation* (Maryknoll, NY: Orbis, 1991), 20; italics mine. It is also important to note as Shawn Copeland does that "slavery neither exhausts nor circumscribes African American experience." See her *Enfleshing Freedom: Body, Race, and Being* (Minneapolis: Fortress Press, 2010), 28.

65. See the hymn by James Weldon Johnson and J. Rosamond Johnson, referred to as the Negro National Anthem, "Lift Every Voice and Sing," in *Songs of Zion* (Nashville: Abingdon, 1981), 32.

66. Callahan, *Talking Book*, 57.

67. Wyatt Tee Walker, *The Soul of Black Worship* (New York: Martin Luther King Fellows, 1984), 47.

68. Work, *Folk Song*, 16.

69. Johnson and Johnson, *Books of American Negro Spirituals*, 13.

70. See Orlando Patterson, *Slavery and Social Death: A Comparative Study* (Cambridge: Harvard University Press, 1982).

71. Thurman, *Deep River*, 35.

72. Callahan, *Talking Book*, 62.

73. Work, *Folk Song*, 27.

74. Thurman, *Deep River*, 14.

75. Work, *Folk Song*, 7–8.

76. See Du Bois, *Souls of Black Folk*. I am grateful for the work of Audrey Thompson who focuses on these sounds in her study of black preaching. See her PhD dissertation, "'Til Earth and Heaven Ring: A Theological Theory of the Sense of Sound in the Black Preaching Event of the Word," Princeton Theological Seminary, 2010.

77. Du Bois, *Souls of Black Folk*, 275.

78. Cone, *Spirituals and the Blues*, 31.

79. Lovell, *Black Song*, xiv.

80. Paul Dunbar, "The Poet and His Song," http://www.dunbarsite.org/gallery/ThePoetandHisSong.asp.

81. Du Bois, *Souls of Black Folk*, 264.

82. Don Saliers and Emily Saliers, *A Song to Sing, A Life to Live: Reflections on Music as Spiritual Practice* (San Francisco: Jossey-Bass, 2005), xv.

83. Work, *Folk Song*, 20.

84. Lovell, *Black Song*, 74.

85. Troeger, *Wonder Reborn*, 47.

86. William B. McClain, *Come Sunday: The Liturgy of Zion* (Nashville: Abingdon, 1990), 55.

87. Bernice Johnson Reagon, *If You Don't Go: Don't Hinder Me: The African American Sacred Song Tradition* (Lincoln: University of Nebraska Press, 2001), 75.

88. Shane White and Graham White, *The Sounds of Slavery: Discovering African American History Through Songs, Sermons, and Speech* (Boston: Beacon, 2005), 40.

89. Saliers and Saliers, *Song to Sing*, 37.

90. Work, *Folk Song*, 17.

91. Ibid.

92. Paul Jeffrey, "Out of the Rubble: Haiti's Long-Term Needs," *Christian Century* 127, no. 6 (March 23, 2010): 13.

93. Thurman, *Deep River*, 39.

94. See the poem "The Gift to Sing," in James Weldon Johnson, *Complete Poems*, ed. Sondra K. Wilson (New York: Penguin, 2000), 136.

95. Lovell, *Black Song*, 37.

96. Cone, *Spirituals and the Blues*, 30.

97. Riggins Earl, *Dark Symbols, Obscure Signs: God, Self, and Community in the Slave Mind* (Maryknoll, NY: Orbis, 1993), 71.

98. Cone, *Spirituals and the Blues*, 30.

99. Genovese, *Roll, Jordan, Roll*, 236.

100. Johnson, *God's Trombones*, 4.

101. Kirk-Duggan, *Exorcizing Evil*, 60.

102. Genovese, *Roll, Jordan, Roll*, 257.

103. Albert Raboteau, "'The Blood of the Martyrs is the Seed of Faith': Suffering in the Christianity of American Slaves," in *The Courage to Hope: From Black Suffering to Human Redemption,* ed. Quinton Hosford Dixie and Cornel West (Boston: Beacon, 1999), 26.

104. Ibid., 26. For other stories about the suppression of singing and preaching, see Dena Epstein, *Sinful Tunes and Spirituals: Black Folk Music to the Civil War* (Urbana: University of Illinois Press, 1977), 229–32.

105. Raboteau, "Blood of the Martyrs," 28.

106. Bernice Johnson Reagon, quoted in Arthur C. Jones, *Wade in the Water: The Wisdom of the Spirituals* (Maryknoll, NY: Orbis, 1993), 22.

107. Quoted in Jon Michael Spencer, *Protest and Praise: The Sacred Music of Black Religion* (Minneapolis: Fortress Press, 1990), 13.

108. Ibid., 6.

109. Cone, *Spirituals and the Blues*, 24; for other forms of resistance such as running away, theft, or arson, see 23–31.

110. Copeland, *Enfleshing Freedom*, 38.

111. Lovell, *Black Song*, 190.

112. Ibid., 191.

113. Spencer, *Protest and Praise*, 17. For an account of Harriet Tubman's use of the "mask," see John Blassingame, *The Slave Community: Plantation Life in the Antebellum South* (New York: Oxford University Press, 1979), 458–59.

114. Peter Paris, "When Feeling Like a Motherless Child," in *Lament: Reclaiming Practices in Pulpit, Pew, and Public Square,* ed. Sally A. Brown and Patrick D. Miller (Louisville: Westminster John Knox, 2005), 113.

115. Blassingame, *Slave Community*, 145.

116. White and White, *Sounds of Slavery*, 51.

117. Genovese, *Roll, Jordan, Roll*, 269.

118. White and White, *Sounds of Slavery*, xiii.

119. Cleveland and McClain, "A Historical Account of the Negro Spiritual," 73.

120. Callahan, *Talking Book*, 70.

121. Johnson and Johnson, *Books of American Negro Spirituals,* 28. Cf. Lovell, *Black Song*, 67; Work, *Folk Song,* 38; Callahan, *Talking Book*, 70.

122. Melva Costen, *In Spirit and In Truth: The Music of African American Worship* (Louisville: Westminster John Knox, 2004), 131.

123. For a description of the ring shout, see William Francis Allen, Charles Pickard Ware, and Lucy McKim Garrison, *Slave Songs of the United States: The Classic 1867 Anthology* (New York: Dover, 1995 [1867]), xiii–xv.

124. Callahan, *Talking Book*, 62.

125. These words come from a song sung by Billie Holiday, "Strange Fruit," written in 1937 by Abel Meeropol, a Jewish schoolteacher in New York.

126. Raboteau, "Blood of the Martyrs," 35.

127. Cone, *Spirituals and the Blues*, 31.

128. Paul Gilroy, *The Black Atlantic: Modernity and Double Consciousness* (Cambridge: Harvard University Press, 1993), 189.

129. See Johnson and Johnson, "Lift Every Voice and Sing."

130. Toni Morrison, "The Site of Memory," in *Inventing the Truth: The Art and Craft of Memoir,* ed. William Zinsser (Boston: Houghton Mifflin, 1995), 98.

131. Howard Thurman, *Disciplines of the Spirit* (Richmond, IN: Friends United, 1963), 64.

132. See Raboteau, "Blood of the Martyrs."

133. Ibid., 37.

134. Du Bois, *Souls of Black Folk*, 264.

135. Douglas John Hall, "Preaching Reconciliation in a World of Long Memories," *Journal for Preachers* 26, no. 2 (Lent 2003): 11.

136. Houston Baker, *Critical Memory Public Spheres, African American Writing, and Blacks and Sons in America* (Athens: University of Georgia Press, 2001), 72.

137. Saint Augustine, *Confessions,* Book IX.12, trans. R. S. Pine-Coffin (New York: Penguin, 1961), 202.

138. Fred Craddock, "Preaching: An Appeal to Memory," in *What's the Matter with Preaching?* ed. Mike Graves (Louisville: Westminster John Knox, 2004), 60.

139. Copeland, *Enfleshing Freedom*, 3.

140. Johnson and Johnson, "Lift Every Voice and Sing."

141. James Cone, "Strange Fruit: The Cross and the Lynching Tree," *The African American Pulpit* 11, no. 2 (Spring 2008): 18–26.

142. Raboteau, "Blood of the Martyrs," 37.

143. Copeland, *Enfleshing Freedom*, 129.

144. See Cleophus J. LaRue, "The Exodus as Paradigmatic Text in the African American Community," in *Reclaiming the Imagination: The Exodus as Paradigmatic Narrative for Preaching,* ed. David Fleer and Dave Bland (St. Louis: Chalice, 2009), 119–28.

145. Callahan, *Talking Book*, 56.

146. Craddock, "Preaching," 64.

147. Gilroy, *Black Atlantic*, 200.

148. Toni Morrison, *Beloved* (New York: Vintage, 2004 [1987]), 102–04.

149. Robert O'Meally and Geneviève Fabre call the black bards "historians without portfolio." See "Introduction," in *History and Memory in African American Culture,* eds. Geneviève Fabre and Robert O'Meally (New York: Oxford University Press, 1994), 150–63.

150. Martin Luther King Jr., "The Drum Major Instinct," in *A Testament of Hope: The Essential Writings and Speeches of Martin Luther King, Jr.,* ed. James M. Washington (San Francisco: HarperCollins, 1986), 259–67.

151. Morrison, "Site of Memory," 95.

152. Callahan, *Talking Book*, 56.

153. Johnson and Johnson, *Books of American Negro Spirituals,* 13.

154. Samuel D. Proctor, *How Shall They Hear? Effective Preaching for Vital Faith* (Valley Forge: Judson, 1992), 81.

155. Jones, *Jazz of Preaching*, 21.

156. Proctor, *How Shall They Hear?* 99.

157. Morrison, *Beloved,* 273.

158. David Blight, "If You Don't Tell It Like It Was, It Can Never Be as It Ought to Be," in *Slavery and Public History: The Tough Stuff of American Memory,* ed. James Oliver Horton and Lois E. Horton (New York: New Press, 2006), 33.

159. David Fleer and Dave Bland, "Introduction," in *Reclaiming the Imagination: The Exodus as Paradigmatic Narrative for Preaching*, ed. David Fleer and Dave Bland (St. Louis: Chalice, 2009), 3.

160. Maurice Halbwachs, *On Collective Memory*, ed. and trans. Lewis A. Coser (Chicago: University of Chicago Press, 1992), 88.

161. Fred Craddock, "Funds in the Memory Bank," Sprunt Lectures presented at Union Theological Seminary and Presbyterian School of Christian Education, Richmond, VA, 1991.

162. Lisa Lamb, "To Remember Well Together: Preaching in Ethnically Diverse Congregations," *Word & World* 28, no. 4 (Fall 2008): 424–32.

163. Karen Fields, "What One Cannot Remember Mistakenly," in Fabre and O'Meally, eds., *History and Memory*, 161.

164. Miroslav Volf, *The End of Memory: Remembering Rightly in a Violent World* (Grand Rapids: Eerdmans, 2006), 21.

165. Gilroy, *Black Atlantic*, 71.

166. Don E. Saliers, *Worship Come to Its Senses* (Nashville: Abingdon, 1996), 68.

2. Hear the Word of the Lord: The Content of *Spiritual* Preaching

1. James Forbes, *The Holy Spirit and Preaching* (Nashville: Abingdon, 1989), 19.

2. John R. Levison, *Filled with the Spirit* (Grand Rapids: Eerdmans, 2009), 88.

3. Ibid., 99.

4. W. E. B. Du Bois, *The Souls of Black Folk* (New York: Penguin, 1969 [1903]), 211.

5. Donald H. Matthews, *Honoring the Ancestors: An African Cultural Interpretation of Black Religion and Literature* (New York: Oxford University Press, 1998), 66.

6. Bernice Johnson Reagon, *If You Don't Go, Don't Hinder Me: The African American Sacred Song Tradition* (Lincoln: University of Nebraska Press, 2001), 68.

7. The myth of High John De Conqueror affirms this. For the entire story, see Zora Neale Hurston, *The Sanctified Church* (Berkeley: Turtle Island, 1983), 69–78.

8. A journalist during the Civil War says this about a particular black regiment; see Reagon, *If You Don't Go*, 80.

9. William Turner, "Foreword," in Jon Michael Spencer, *Sacred Symphony: The Chanted Sermon of the Black Preacher* (New York: Greenwood, 1987), xi.

10. James Weldon Johnson and J. Rosamond Johnson, *The Books of American Negro Spirituals* (New York: Da Capo, 1977 [1969; orig. 2 vols., 1925, 1926]), 11–12.

11. Two spirituals that have a greater focus on the Spirit are "Every Time I Feel the Spirit" and "I'm Gonna Sing." Some others that include mention of the Spirit are "There is a Balm in Gilead," "The Old Ship of Zion," and "Walk in Jerusalem Jus' like John."

12. James Earl Massey, "Faith and Christian Life in the African-American Spirituals," in *God the Holy Trinity: Reflections on Christian Faith and Practice*, ed. Timothy George (Grand Rapids: Baker Academic, 2006), 65.

13. Matthews, *Honoring the Ancestors*, 65. John Lovell notes that for folk oral cultures, "sound forms the basis of reality in the universe." See John Lovell Jr., *Black Song: The Forge and the Flame* (New York: Macmillan, 1972), 5. See n.8, above, to find reference to High John.

14. Some passages to explore the interaction of Spirit and sound are Luke 1:39-56; John 3:1-15; and Acts 2:1-13. Cf. Audrey Thompson, "'Til Earth and Heaven Ring: A

Theological Theory of the Sense of Sound in the Black Preaching Event of the Word,"
(Ph.D. diss., Princeton Theological Seminary, 2010).

15. Reagon, *If You Don't Go*, 42.

16. Ibid., 73.

17. Frederick Douglass, *My Bondage and My Freedom* (New York: Dover, 1969
[1855]), 99.

18. Walter Pitts, *Old Ship of Zion: The Afro-Baptist Ritual in the African Diaspora*
(New York: Oxford University Press, 1993), 130.

19. Arthur Jones, *Wade in the Water: The Wisdom of the Spirituals* (Maryknoll,
NY: Orbis, 1993), xvi.

20. Ibid., 15.

21. Robert Beckford, *Jesus Dub: Theology, Music and Social Change* (New York:
Routledge, 2006), 15.

22. See Jeremy S. Begbie, *Theology, Music and Time* (Cambridge: Cambridge University Press, 2000); Don E. Saliers, *Music and Theology* (Nashville: Abingdon, 2007).

23. Stephen H. Webb, *The Divine Voice: Christian Proclamation and the Theology
of Sound* (Grand Rapids: Brazos, 2004), 32.

24. Lovell, *Black Song*, 130.

25. Reagon, *If You Don't Go*, 68.

26. Kirk Byron Jones, *The Jazz of Preaching: How to Preach with Great Freedom
and Joy* (Nashville: Abingdon, 2004), 19–20.

27. George C. L. Cummings, "The Slave Narratives as a Source of Black Theological Discourse: The Spirit and Eschatology," in *Cut Loose Your Stammering Tongue:
Black Theology in the Slave Narratives*, ed. Dwight N. Hopkins and George C. L. Cummings (Louisville: Westminster John Knox, 2003), 53–54.

28. James Cone, *The Spirituals and the Blues: An Interpretation* (Maryknoll, NY:
Orbis, 1991), 17.

29. Howard Thurman, *Deep River and the Negro Speaks of Life and Death* (Richmond, IN: Friends United, 1975), 13–14.

30. Ibid., 37–38.

31. Wyatt Tee Walker, *"Somebody's Calling My Name": Black Sacred Music and
Social Change* (Valley Forge: Judson, 1979), 46.

32. Pauli Murray, *Dark Testament and Other Poems* (Norwalk, CT: Silvermine,
1970).

33. Du Bois, *Souls of Black Folk*, 267.

34. Raboteau, *Slave Religion*, 262.

35. John Lovell purports that death was a mask. He says, "Although those creators
used death as a figure of speech (as their ancestors had done), they were young men and
women who thought very little about literal dying. No literal death could have been
worse to them than slavery. . . . To wear the mask of death, as, once more, their singing ancestors had often done, was to open a free sky to plan, without penalty from the
oppressor, the secret ways to become free, and more important, to do something constructive with their lives." See Lovell, *Black Song*, 112.

36. Massey, "Faith and Christian Life," 59.

37. Cone, *Spirituals and the Blues*, 43.

38. Ibid., 35.

39. Thurman, *Deep River*, 94.

40. For this nuanced perspective, see Cone, *Spirituals and the Blues*, 63–64; cf. Arthur C. Jones, "Upon This Rock: The Foundational Influence of the Spirituals," in *The Triumph of the Soul: Cultural and Psychological Aspects of African American Music*, ed. Ferdinand Jones and Arthur C. Jones (Westport, CT: Praeger, 2001), 3–34.

41. Begbie, *Theology, Music and Time*, 98.

42. Du Bois, *Souls of Black Folk*, 274.

43. Thurman, *Deep River*, 24.

44. Albert Raboteau, *A Sorrowful Joy* (New York: Paulist, 2002).

45. Thurman, *Deep River*, 28.

46. William B. McClain, *Come Sunday: The Liturgy of Zion* (Nashville: Abingdon, 1990), 13.

47. Thurman, *Deep River*, 32.

48. Lovell, *Black Song*, 6.

49. Cone, *Spirituals and the Blues*, 86.

50. Du Bois, *Souls of Black Folk*, 269.

51. For a discussion about the loss of eschatology in preaching today, see Thomas G. Long, *Preaching from Memory to Hope* (Louisville: Westminster John Knox, 2009), 111–32.

52. Thurman, *Deep River*, 36.

53. Ibid., 25.

54. Peter Paris, "When Feeling Like a Motherless Child," in *Lament: Reclaiming Practices in Pulpit, Pew, and Public Square*, ed. Sally A. Brown and Patrick D. Miller (Louisville: Westminster John Knox, 2005), 113.

55. Jones, "Upon This Rock," 9.

56. Walker, *"Somebody's Calling My Name,"* 54.

57. Hurston, *Sanctified Church*, 80.

58. Evans Crawford, *The Hum: Call and Response in African American Preaching* (Nashville: Abingdon, 1995), 71.

59. Gardner Taylor, *How Shall They Preach* (Elgin, IL: Progressive Baptist Pub. House, 1977), 91.

60. Lovell, *Black Song*, 120.

61. These three categories are known as the rhetorical proofs in ancient Greek rhetoric. See Lucy Lind Hogan and Robert Reid, *Connecting with the Congregation: Rhetoric and the Art of Preaching* (Nashville: Abingdon, 1999).

62. Bruce Rosenberg, *Can These Bones Live? The Art of the American Folk Preacher*, rev. ed. (Urbana: University of Illinois Press, 1988), 23.

63. See Don Geiger, *The Sound, Sense, and Performance of Literature* (Glenview, IL: Scott, Foresman, 1963).

64. Walter Brueggemann, *Finally Comes the Poet: Daring Speech for Proclamation* (Minneapolis: Fortress Press, 1989), 3.

65. Cleophus J. LaRue, *I Believe I'll Testify: The Art of African American Preaching* (Louisville: Westminster John Knox, 2011), 93; italics mine.

66. Ibid., 83.

67. Hurston, *Sanctified Church*, 50–51.

68. LaRue, *I Believe I'll Testify*, 95.

69. James Earl Massey, *Stewards of the Story: The Task of Preaching* (Louisville: Westminster John Knox, 2006), 42.

70. Long, *Preaching from Memory to Hope*, 37.

71. Lauri Ramey, "The Theology of the Lyric Tradition in African American Spirituals," *Journal of the American Academy of Religion* 70, no. 2 (2002): 355.

72. Paul Scott Wilson, *Setting Words on Fire: Putting God at the Center of the Sermon* (Nashville: Abingdon, 2008).

73. Thomas Troeger, "Keeping in Touch with God: Why Homiletics Is Always More than Method," in *Purposes of Preaching,* ed. Jana Childers (St. Louis: Chalice, 2004), 113–30.

74. James Kay writes, "Preachers signify the divine promises, but only the divine Promisor can make them significant to the hearers." See his essay "Preacher as Messenger of Hope," in *Slow of Speech, Unclean Lips: Contemporary Images of Preaching Identity,* ed. Robert Stephen Reid (Eugene, OR: Cascade, 2010), 30.

75. LaRue, *I Believe I'll Testify*, 60.

76. James H. Harris, *Preaching Liberation*, Fortress Resources for Preaching (Minneapolis: Fortress Press, 1995), 24.

77. "Without Him," in *Hymns of the Spirit*, ed. Connor B. Hall (Cleveland: Pathway, 1969), 107.

78. See the corpus of homiletical literature by Paul Scott Wilson.

79. Paul Scott Wilson, *The Practice of Preaching,* rev. ed. (Nashville: Abingdon, 2007), 49.

80. Peter J. Gomes, *The Scandalous Gospel of Jesus: What's So Good about the Good News?* (New York: HarperCollins, 2007), 221.

81. Ibid., 220.

82. Paul Scott Wilson, *Broken Words: Reflections on the Craft of Preaching* (Nashville: Abingdon, 2004), 152.

83. Samuel Proctor, *How Shall They Hear? Effective Preaching for Vital Faith* (Valley Forge: Judson, 1992), 17, 87.

84. Ibid., 85.

85. Ibid., 97.

86. Charles Campbell, *The Word Before the Powers: An Ethic of Preaching* (Louisville: Westminster John Knox, 2002), 119–27.

87. Ibid., 120.

88. LaRue, *I Believe I'll Testify*, 96.

89. Kay, "Preacher as Messenger of Hope," 31.

3. Prophesy to the Bones: Generating Hope through Preaching

1. See Barack Obama, *The Audacity of Hope: Thoughts on Reclaiming the American Dream* (New York: Three Rivers, 2006).

2. See President Obama's speech after the New Hampshire primary vote at http://www.nytimes.com/2008/01/08/us/politics/08text-obama.html.

3. Thomas G. Long, *The Witness of Preaching* (Louisville: Westminster John Knox, 1989), 86–91.

4. See Max Turner, *The Holy Spirit and Spiritual Gifts in the New Testament Church and Today* (Peabody, MA: Hendrickson, 1996), 7–20.

5. Charles L. Bartow, *God's Human Speech: A Practical Theology of Proclamation* (Grand Rapids: Eerdmans, 1997).

6. See J. L. Austin, *How To Do Things with Words* (Cambridge: Harvard University Press, 1975).

7. Henry H. Mitchell, *Black Preaching: The Recovery of a Powerful Art* (Nashville: Abingdon, 1990), 130.

8. Kenyatta R. Gilbert, *The Journey and Promise of African American Preaching* (Minneapolis: Fortress Press, 2011), 4.

9. Eschatology is known as the Christian doctrine of the last things.

10. Paul Scott Wilson, *Broken Words: Reflections on the Craft of Preaching* (Nashville: Abingdon, 2004), 152.

11. Thomas G. Long, *Preaching from Memory to Hope* (Louisville: Westminster John Knox, 2009), xv.

12. James Forbes, *The Holy Spirit and Preaching* (Nashville: Abingdon, 1989), 74.

13. For the Jewish connection between the Spirit and eschatological salvific future of a people, see Isa. 11:2; 32:15-16; 34:16; 42:1; 44:3; 59:21; 61:1. Also, see Ezek. 11:19; 18:31; 36:26-27; 37:1-14.

14. James D. G. Dunn, *The Theology of Paul the Apostle* (Grand Rapids: Eerdmans, 1998), 436. Cf. Rom. 5:2-5; 8:23-25; 15:13; Gal. 5:5; 1 Cor. 13:7, 13.

15. Cf. 2 Cor. 1:22; 5:5.

16. Gordon Fee, *God's Empowering Presence: The Holy Spirit in the Letters of Paul* (Peabody, MA: Hendrickson, 1994), 571.

17. Martin Luther King Jr., "Eulogy for the Martyred Children," in *A Testament of Hope: The Essential Writings and Speeches of Martin Luther King Jr.*, ed. James M. Washington (San Francisco: HarperCollins, 1986), 222.

18. Dale P. Andrews, *Practical Theology for Black Churches: Bridging Black Theology and African American Folk Religion* (Louisville: Westminster John Knox, 2002), 47.

19. Ibid., 48.

20. Gayraud Wilmore, quoted in James Evans, *We Have Been Believers: An African-American Systematic Theology* (Minneapolis: Fortress Press, 1992), 152.

21. Long, *Preaching from Memory to Hope*, 123.

22. Cheryl Bridges Johns, "Eschatology," in *The New Interpreter's Handbook of Preaching*, ed. Paul Scott Wilson, et al. (Nashville: Abingdon, 2008), 460.

23. Cornel West with David Ritz, *Brother West, Living and Loving Out Loud: A Memoir* (New York: Smiley, 2009), 6; and Cornel West, "The Spirituals as Lyrical Poetry," in *The Cornel West Reader* (New York: Basic, 1999), 463, respectively.

24. Long, *Preaching from Memory to Hope*, 124.

25. See A. Elaine Brown Crawford, *Hope in the Holler: A Womanist Theology* (Louisville: Westminster John Knox, 2002).

26. James Weldon Johnson, *God's Trombones: Seven Negro Sermons in Verse* (New York: Penguin, 1927), 3.

27. Jürgen Moltmann, *The Way of Jesus Christ: Christology in Messianic Dimensions*, trans. Margaret Kohl (Minneapolis: Fortress Press, 1993 [1990]), 78, 94.

28. Jürgen Moltmann, *The Spirit of Life: A Universal Affirmation*, trans. Margaret Kohl (Minneapolis: Fortress Press, 1994), 17–18.

29. Ibid., 62.

30. Andrews, *Practical Theology for Black Churches*, 44.

31. James Cone, "Strange Fruit: The Cross and the Lynching Tree," *The African American Pulpit* 11, no. 2 (Spring 2008): 24. Cf. Cone, *The Cross and the Lynching Tree* (Maryknoll, NY: Orbis, 2011).

32. Johnson, *God's Trombones*, 42.

33. Mary Catherine Hilkert, *Naming Grace: Preaching and the Sacramental Imagination* (New York: Continuum, 1997), 116.

34. See my sermon, "Death Threat," *The Princeton Seminary Bulletin* 28, no. 3 (2007): 244–50.

35. James Cone, *The Spirituals and the Blues: An Interpretation* (Maryknoll, NY: Orbis, 1991), 50.

36. James F. Kay, "He Descended into Hell," *Word & World* 31, no. 1 (Winter 2011): 23.

37. Ibid., 25–26.

38. Katie Geneva Cannon, *Teaching Preaching: Isaac Rufus Clark and Black Sacred Rhetoric* (New York: Continuum, 2002), 179.

39. Cleophus J. LaRue, *The Heart of Black Preaching* (Louisville: Westminster John Knox, 2000), 112.

40. Hilkert, *Naming Grace*, 83.

41. David G. Buttrick, *Preaching Jesus: An Exercise in Homiletic Theology* (Minneapolis: Fortress Press, 1988), 51.

42. Thomas G. Long, *Accompany Them with Singing: The Christian Funeral* (Louisville: Westminster John Knox, 2009), 44.

43. N. T. Wright, *Surprised by Hope: Rethinking Heaven, the Resurrection, and the Mission of the Church* (San Francisco: HarperOne, 2008), 191.

44. Jürgen Moltmann, *Theology of Hope: On the Ground and the Implications of a Christian Eschatology*, trans. James W. Leitch (Minneapolis: Fortress Press, 1993 [1967]), 22, 34–35, 288–90.

45. Ibid., 22.

46. Richard Lischer, *A Theology of Preaching: The Dynamics of the Gospel,* rev. ed. (Eugene: Wipf and Stock, 2001), 29.

47. Ibid.

48. This statement is by my New Testament colleague, George Parsenios.

49. Desmond Tutu, responding to Ted Koppel on *Nightline* in the 1980s about whether the situation in South Africa was hopeless, said, "Of course it is hopeless from a human point of view. But we believe in the resurrection, and so we are prisoners of hope." See James F. Kay, "Preaching in Advent," *Journal for Preachers* 13, no. 1 (Advent 1989): 11–16.

50. Pauli Murray, *Dark Testament and Other Poems* (Norwalk, CT: Silvermine, 1970).

51. Paul Scott Wilson, *The Practice of Preaching,* rev. ed. (Nashville: Abingdon, 2007), 49.

52. David Buttrick, *Preaching the New and Now* (Louisville: Westminster John Knox, 1998), 23.

53. Ibid., 22, 66.

54. For one such approach, see Paul Scott Wilson, *Preaching and Homiletical Theory* (St. Louis: Chalice, 2004), 73–100.

55. James H. Harris, *Preaching Liberation*, Fortress Resources for Preaching (Minneapolis: Fortress Press, 1995), 52.

56. Gardner C. Taylor, *How Shall They Preach?* (Elgin, IL: Progressive Baptist Pub. House, 1977), 104–06.

57. William B. McClain, *Come Sunday: The Liturgy of Zion* (Nashville: Abingdon, 1990), 69–70.

58. Cas J. A. Vos, "Preaching as a Language of Hope," in *Preaching as a Language of Hope*, ed. Cas Vos, et al. (Pretoria: Protea Book House, 2007), 11.

59. Cornel West speaks of "hope on a tightrope" due to hope being grounded in struggle while not being betrayed by utopian visions of a better future that do not take into consideration real work moving toward concrete manifestations of a just and loving world. West represents the spiritual theology that is heavenly-minded and earthly-good. See his *Hope on a Tightrope: Words & Wisdom* (Carlsbad, CA: Smiley, 2008).

60. Lischer, *A Theology of Preaching*, 28.

61. Thomas Troeger, *Imaging a Sermon* (Nashville: Abingdon, 1990), 17–18.

62. Richard Lischer, *The Preacher King: Martin Luther King Jr. and the Word That Moved America* (New York: Oxford University Press, 1995), 122.

63. Charles L. Campbell, *The Word Before the Powers: An Ethic of Preaching* (Louisville: Westminster John Knox, 2002), 186.

64. Wilson, *Broken Words*, 152.

65. Luke A. Powery, "Tracks of My Tears," *Princeton Seminary Bulletin* 30 (2009): 16–21.

66. Campbell, *Word Before the Powers*, 123–25.

67. J. Alfred Smith, "Foundations of Our Faith," in *Power in the Pulpit: How America's Most Effective Black Preachers Prepare Their Sermons*, ed. Cleophus J. LaRue (Louisville: Westminster John Knox, 2002), 143.

68. Jan Hermelink, "The Theological Understanding of Preaching Hope," in Vos et al., eds., *Preaching as a Language of Hope*, 41.

69. This story can be found at http://news.bbc.co.uk/2/hi/africa/662472.stm.

70. Howard Thurman, "The Growing Edge," in *The Mood of Christmas* (Richmond, IN: Friends United, 1983 [1973]), 23.

71. Long, *Preaching from Memory to Hope*, 124.

72. Hilkert, *Naming Grace*, 53.

73. Lischer, *Preacher King*, 120–21; italics mine.

74. Buttrick, *Preaching the New and Now*, 100.

75. Ibid., 121.

76. Linda Lee Clader, "Metaphor and Figures of Speech," in Wilson et al., eds., *New Interpreters' Handbook of Preaching*, 193.

77. Ibid., 194.

78. Albert Raboteau, "'The Blood of the Martyrs is the Seed of Faith': Suffering in the Christianity of American Slaves," in *The Courage to Hope: From Black Suffering to Human Redemption,* ed. Quinton Hosford Dixie and Cornel West (Boston: Beacon, 1999), 34.

79. Martin Luther King, Jr., "I See the Promised Land," in *A Testament of Hope*, ed. Washington, 286.

80. Johnson, *God's Trombones,* 4–5.

81. Walter Brueggemann, *Finally Comes the Poet: Daring Speech for Proclamation* (Minneapolis: Fortress Press, 1989).

82. Zora Neale Hurston, *The Sanctified Church* (Berkeley: Turtle Island, 1983), 50.

83. See Paul Scott Wilson, *Four Pages of a Sermon: A Guide to Biblical Preaching* (Nashville: Abingdon, 1999).

84. Elaine Brown Crawford, *Hope in the Holler: A Womanist Theology* (Louisville: Westminster John Knox, 2002), 109.

85. Cleophus J. LaRue, *I Believe I'll Testify: The Art of African American Preaching* (Louisville: Westminster John Knox, 2011), 95–96.

86. Henry H. Mitchell, *Celebration and Experience in Preaching* (Nashville: Abingdon, 1990), 25.

87. Mitchell, *Black Preaching*, 21.

88. Gerhard O. Forde, *Theology Is for Proclamation* (Minneapolis: Fortress Press, 1990), 149–50.

89. Teresa Fry Brown, *Weary Throats and New Songs: Black Women Proclaiming God's Word* (Nashville: Abingdon, 2003), 149.

90. Ibid., 154.

91. Wilson, *The Practice of Preaching*, 100.

92. Don E. Saliers, *Worship Come to Its Senses* (Nashville: Abingdon, 1996), 79.

93. Valentino Lassiter, *Martin Luther King in the African American Preaching Tradition* (Cleveland: Pilgrim, 2001), 77.

4. You Shall Live: Reading the Bible for Preaching Hope (and Death)

1. John Levison, *Filled with the Spirit* (Grand Rapids: Eerdmans, 2009), 103.

2. James Forbes, *The Holy Spirit and Preaching* (Nashville: Abingdon, 1989), 100.

3. Paul Scott Wilson, *The Practice of Preaching*, rev. ed. (Nashville: Abingdon, 2007), 49.

4. See the clip of Pastor Freddie Haynes at http://www.youtube.com/watch?v=9LeIlms9HOk.

5. Bruno Chenu, *The Trouble I've Seen: The Big Book of Negro Spirituals*, trans. Eugene V. LaPlante (Valley Forge: Judson, 2003), 145.

6. Wyatt Tee Walker, *"Somebody's Calling My Name": Black Sacred Music and Social Change* (Valley Forge: Judson, 1979), 52–54.

7. John W. Work, *Folk Song of the American Negro* (New York: Negro Universities Press, 1969 [1915]), 36.

8. Donald Matthews, *Honoring the Ancestors: An African Cultural Interpretation of Black Religion and Literature* (New York: Oxford University Press, 1998), 101.

9. James Cone, *The Spirituals and the Blues: An Interpretation* (Maryknoll, NY: Orbis, 1991), 37.

10. James Weldon Johnson, *God's Trombones: Seven Negro Sermons in Verse* (New York: Viking Penguin, 1927), 4.

11. Ibid., 6.

12. Cone, *Spirituals and the Blues*, 37–38.

13. Allen Dwight Callahan, *The Talking Book: African Americans and the Bible* (New Haven: Yale University Press, 2006), xi.

14. Albert Raboteau, *Slave Religion: The 'Invisible Institution' in the Antebellum South* (New York: Oxford University Press, 1978), 243.

15. Renita J. Weems, "Reading *Her Way* through the Struggle: African American Women and the Bible," in *Stony the Road We Trod: African American Biblical Interpretation*, ed. Cain Hope Felder (Minneapolis: Fortress Press, 1991), 61.

16. James Evans, *We Have Been Believers: An African American Systematic Theology* (Minneapolis: Fortress Press, 1992), 52.

17. John Lovell Jr., *Black Song: The Forge and the Flame* (New York: Macmillan, 1972), 262–63.

18. Ibid., 263.

19. Raquel St. Clair, "Interpreting Scripture for the Purpose of Writing a Sermon," *The African American Pulpit* (Summer 2004), http://www.theafricanamericanlectionary.org/pdf/preaching/InterpretingScripture_RachelClair.pdf.

20. Cleophus J. LaRue, *I Believe I'll Testify: The Art of African American Preaching* (Louisville: Westminster John Knox, 2011), 57.

21. See *The Columbia World of Quotations*, ed. Robert Andrews, Mary Biggs, and Michael Seidel (New York: Columbia University Press, 1996).

22. Brian K. Blount, *Cultural Interpretation: Reorienting New Testament Criticism* (Minneapolis: Fortress Press, 1995), 56.

23. Evans, *We Have Been Believers*, 52.

24. Samuel D. Proctor, *How Shall They Hear? Effective Preaching for Vital Faith* (Valley Forge: Judson, 1992), 37.

25. Marvin McMickle, *Shaping the Claim: Moving from Text to Sermon*, Elements of Preaching (Minneapolis: Fortress Press, 2008), 20.

26. Arthur Jones, *Wade in the Water: The Wisdom of the Spirituals* (Maryknoll, NY: Orbis, 1993), 31.

27. Weems, "Reading *Her Way*," 62.

28. William McClain, "African American Preaching and the Bible: Biblical Authority or Biblical Liberalism," *Journal of Religious Thought* 49, no. 2 (Winter/Spring 1992–93): 72–80, http://www.theafricanamericanlectionary.org/pdf/preaching/AfricanAmericanPreachingandtheBible_WilliamMcClain.pdf.

29. Cone, 37.

30. Frank A. Thomas, *They Like to Never Quit Praisin' God: The Role of Celebration in Preaching* (Cleveland: Pilgrim, 1997), 71.

31. Howard Thurman, *Deep River and the Negro Speaks of Life and Death* (Richmond, IN: Friends United, 1975), 15.

32. McClain, "African American Preaching and the Bible."

33. Gardner Taylor, *How Shall They Preach?* (Elgin, IL: Progressive Baptist Pub. House, 1977), 60.

34. Valentino Lassiter, *Martin Luther King in the African American Preaching Tradition* (Cleveland: Pilgrim, 2001), 19. For more about the hermeneutic of God, see Cleophus J. LaRue, *The Heart of Black Preaching* (Louisville: Westminster John Knox, 1999), 18–20; and Warren Stewart, *Interpreting God's Word in Black Preaching* (Valley Forge: Judson, 1984).

35. Blount, *Cultural Interpretation*, 61.

36. Thurman, *Deep River*, 94.

37. Henry H. Mitchell, *Black Preaching: Recovery of a Powerful Art* (Nashville: Abingdon, 1990), 130.

38. Katie Geneva Cannon, *Teaching Preaching: Isaac Rufus Clark and Black Sacred Rhetoric* (New York: Continuum, 2002), 181.

39. Thurman, *Deep River*, 14–15.

40. Lawrence Levine, *Black Culture and Black Consciousness: Afro-American Folk Thought from Slavery to Freedom* (New York: Oxford University Press, 1977), 32–33, 50–51.

41. Dale Andrews, *Practical Theology for Black Churches: Bridging Black Theology and African American Folk Religion* (Louisville: Westminster John Knox, 2002), 19.

42. Barbara Holmes, *Joy Unspeakable: Contemplative Practices of the Black Church* (Minneapolis: Fortress Press, 2004), 137.

43. Evans, *We Have Been Believers*, 46.

44. Marvin McMickle, *Living Water for Thirsty Souls: Unleashing the Power of Exegetical Preaching* (Valley Forge: Judson, 2001), 132–48.

45. Raboteau, *Slave Religion*, 240.

46. Callahan, *The Talking Book*, 190.

47. Charles B. Copher, "Biblical Characters, Events, Places and Images Remembered and Celebrated in Black Worship," *Journal of the Interdenominational Theological Center* 14, nos. 1–2 (Fall/Spring 1986–1987): 80.

48. James Abbington, "Biblical Themes in the R. Nathaniel Dett Collection *Religious Folk-Songs of the Negro* (1927)," in *African Americans and the Bible: Sacred Texts and Social Textures*, ed. Vincent Wimbush (New York: Continuum, 2001), 286–87.

49. Vincent Wimbush, "The Bible and African Americans: An Outline of an Interpretative History," in Felder, ed., *Stony the Road*, 86.

50. Thurman, *Deep River*, 16–17.

51. Ibid., 34.

52. See Douglas B. Sagal, "'Imaginative Insight': Midrash and African-American Preaching," *Judaism* 50, no.1 (Winter 2011): 3–16.

53. Mitchell, *Black Preaching*, 63.

54. Holmes, *Joy Unspeakable*, 120.

55. Abbington, "Biblical Themes," 290.

56. Teresa Fry Brown, *Weary Throats and New Songs: Black Women Proclaiming God's Word* (Nashville: Abingdon, 2003), 150–51.

57. Evans, *We Have Been Believers*, 50.

58. Thurman, *Deep River*, 56.

59. Wimbush, "The Bible and African Americans," 88.

60. Howard Thurman, *The Mood of Christmas* (Richmond, IN: Friends United, 1973), 49–50.

61. Wilson, *Practice of Preaching*, 49. Imagination has been an important topic in homiletics. Due to space I cannot delve further into it, but a few key thinkers on the subject in relation to preaching include: Paul Scott Wilson, Tom Troeger, Charles Rice, Walter Brueggemann, Mary Catherine Hilkert, Anna Carter Florence, and Richard Eslinger.

62. LaRue, *I Believe I'll Testify*, 72.

63. I owe thanks to *The African American Lectionary* for opening up this perspective in fresh ways. Every biblical commentary for that project includes what is called "Descriptive Details," which asks for a sensory exegesis. Also helpful in this regard is the work of Teresa Fry Brown in *Delivering the Sermon: Voice, Body, and Animation in Proclamation* (Minneapolis: Fortress Press, 2008), 55–56, 81.

Index